MATERIAL IMMATERIAL

MATERIAL IMMATERIAL

Botond Bognar

project descriptions by Balázs Bognár

THE NEW WORK OF KENGO KUMA

Princeton Architectural Press | New York

Contents

Acknowledgments

I would like to acknowledge, with much appreciation, the help of my architect son, Balázs Bognár, who, having lived and worked in Japan and knowing much about its architecture, has written all of the project descriptions in this book with skill and insight.

Moreover, I am very grateful to Kengo Kuma and his office for assisting this publication in all of its stages by providing information, and logistical and material support in my travels while I visited and photographed his architecture, and for supplying substantial visual content. Thank you, Kuma San.

In Kuma's office, I am much indebted to Mariko Inaba, the press secretary who was instrumental in assisting with this publication, from the very beginning and in the most substantial way.

In my work, however, I have received help from many people and organizations throughout the years, and herewith I express my sincere gratitude to all of them, including: Fumihiko Maki, Tadao Ando, Toyo Ito, Hiroshi Hara, Riken Yamamoto, Minoru Takeyama, Ryoji Suzuki, Koichi Yasuda, Waro Kishi, Yasumitsu Matsunaga, Kazunari Sakamoto, Koji Yagi, and Atelier Bow Wow, as well as the late Kiyoshi Seike, and Kazuo Shinohara. Thank you all very much indeed.

I must convey my heartfelt gratitude to the offices of Nikken Sekkei, particularly Yoshiaki Ogura, Kiyoshi Sakurai, Tadao Kamei, Shoji Hayashi, and Kunihiro Misu not only for providing an unlimited amount of material but also for their continued collaboration, sharing of expertise, and extensive support for my work throughout the years. I have appreciated it very much.

The architecture department at Tokyo Institute of Technology has, from the very beginning of my work in 1973, provided me with a solid base and much valued assistance. For this, I want to express my appreciation to the previous dean, Kiyoshi Seike, and professors Koji Yagi, Kazunari Sakamoto, Koichi Yasuda, and Yoshiharu Tsukamoto.

My special thanks go to Jumpei Morimoto of the Obayashi Corporation, a longtime friend, and his wife Tatsue, who provided significant help while I lived and worked in Japan.

I have received generous funding from the Research Board of the University of Illinois, without which my work would have been much more difficult to accomplish. I am equally grateful to Professor David Chasco, director of the School of Architecture at the University of Illinois, for his continued support.

Finally, I am indebted to my editors, first of all Laurie Manfra, then Jennifer Thompson, and in earlier times Clare Jacobson, as well as publisher Kevin Lippert, for their dedicated, expert work in the production of this book. Special thanks must also go to this book's designer Paul Wagner, who, understanding the nature of the work, designed each page in the spirit of Kuma's architecture with skill, dedication, and artistry.

This book is dedicated to my wife Binky and sons Balázs, Zsolt, and Bálint, who, in many invaluable ways, are always involved in the work I do.

Introduction

Kengo Kuma

Princeton Architectural Press published a collection of my work five years ago. In my opening remarks, I declared, "My ultimate aim is to 'erase' architecture, because I believe that a building should become one with its surroundings." Fundamentally, my position is the same; however, some changes have taken place in the nuances of my approach. I have started to doubt whether buildings should really disappear into the environment and become completely invisible. One thing that triggered this shift was my losing a number of competitions. In my designs, I tried to erase the building from the landscape. This was the case for the Nam June Paik Museum in Korea in 2003 and the Museum of the History of Polish Jews in 2005. We fared decently during the selection process, but in the end we did not win. We calmly compared the winning design to ours, and it seemed the sponsors did not want architecture that "disappeared." We finally realized the obvious fact that the sponsors wanted a piece of architecture that made a strong statement, since they were spending a large amount of money to build it.

Studying the winning designs in a variety of competitions, we found that this trend has been growing stronger since the completion of the Guggenheim Museum in Bilbao in 1998. The architecture of Frank Gehry opened a new horizon in that it introduced a unique way of producing architecture with monumental sculptural form. Many people welcomed this methodology. Tourists in particular had a love affair with this building. This single piece of architecture brought about dramatic change in the image of the city. This phenomenon, named the Bilbao Effect, ushered in a boom in which cities around the world introduced spectacular architecture for the sake of revitalization. Zaha Hadid was one of the most successful architects to take advantage of this. In fact, we lost to her in a number of competitions.

Naturally, winning competitions is not the only objective of architects, and losing gives us the opportunity to critique the trends of the times. We must, however, be humble enough to listen to what people want. I believe that superior architecture is achieved through a sense of humility toward contemporary movements, and, because of that humility, it survives beyond the current age. Whatever the era, people don't want buildings to which they have devoted a large amount of resources and energy to merely ebb into their surroundings; this is an extremely natural attitude. Still, my aversion to architecture that, I feel, is in conflict with its environment has not changed: I do not intend to retract my desire to "erase" architecture. This raises the question of how to attain balance between the desires of those who commission contemporary work and my own philosophy of architecture. Since the publication of my first book, I have continued to think about what position my architecture should occupy between these two points of view, which appear opposed at first glance.

When I was working on the Chokkura Plaza and Shelter in 2006, I felt that I had come up with part of the answer. I was commissioned to design a public square on a site in the southern part of Utsunomiya, in Tochigi Prefecture. On one side of the site was an old rice storehouse constructed out of Oya stone. We proposed that this building be preserved and that a new building be constructed on the opposite side using the same stone. Our goal was to facilitate a dialogue between the two structures and, in turn, establish a new public plaza between the old and new buildings.

Oya stone is cut from a quarry very near this site. It is a type of tuff, formed as the ash from a volcanic eruption solidifies. Tuff is known for being porous, soft, and fragile compared to granite, marble, and other types of stone frequently used in buildings. What is more, it contains numerous fragments in which the ash is not completely transformed into stone; these areas, indicated by a brownish discoloration, are especially soft. The fragile nature of this stone has been on my mind for some time. Stone is supposed to be strong, rigid, and heavy; however, Oya stone does not have these qualities. It can even be said to be defective as stone, but I see its weakness as its charm.

There is another architect who was attracted to this stone in the same way that I am: Frank Lloyd Wright. When he was to design the Imperial Hotel, in front of the Imperial Palace compound in Tokyo, he asked the construction company to gather all stones available for building. Wright chose Oya stone, and the construction company and local architects working with him were bewildered. With an abundant supply of beautiful granite, marble, and sandstone in the country, it seemed very odd to use a weak stone, full of defects—normally used only for local storehouses—to build a high-class hotel to represent the nation of Japan.

Wright was a great architect, and I often think of him because he was one of the first to challenge architecture as a box; however, his early works were also closed, boxlike structures, similar to the work of other architects of his age. Initially, he was bound by the classical methods of design, in use since the ages of the Greeks and Romans, in which abstract, geometric forms were in conflict with the surrounding natural environment. Two experiences led Wright to change the direction of his architecture. The first was his discovery of Japanese woodblock prints (ukiyo-e), which he became interested in around 1890. In particular, he was strongly attracted to the ukiyo-e of Ando Hiroshige. Wright was greatly influenced by Hiroshige's ability to express the three-dimensionality of space through multiple transparent layers. This method of spatial representation was in stark contrast to the use of perspective as a means to express depth in Western paintings. Wright's admiration of Hiroshige's evocation of space in ukiyo-e led him on a quest to find similar techniques in architecture. He started to head in the direction of overlapping and reconciling exterior and interior spaces in a jointly shared area. This he could make happen by breaking down the thick walls that previously separated them.

The other experience that triggered his new exploration was an encounter with authentic Japanese architecture. He saw his first example of it at the 1893 World's Columbian Exposition in Chicago. He was overwhelmed by the beautiful wood copy of the Byodoin Temple in Uji, built by carpenters dispatched from Japan. The building had a frame construction, with thin pillars, and it was completely open to the environment; as such, it was quite unlike Western buildings, typically supported by heavy walls and closed off from their surroundings. Here, interior space continued toward the outside, joining with the exterior beneath the extensive eaves. Wright's architecture decisively changed after coming face-to-face with this Japanese style, and he ventured toward more open forms in his architecture, in which an extended roof was always a dominant element.

These two episodes were significant not just for Wright; the transparent and overlapping spatial matrix he created in response had considerable influence on European architects, and they represented an important step toward launching modern architecture.

Building a hotel that had to be luxurious and provide complete privacy using a fragile stone was a challenge that could even be called foolhardy, but Wright did not stop there. He had a variety of holes drilled and carved into the stone in an attempt to make it appear even weaker and more fragile. His work was criticized as being decorative, superficial, and too characteristic of the nineteenth century. By no means for mere decoration, these holes represented a no-holds-barred intention by Wright, and the power of his determination had a strong impact on people then and continues to affect us today. In the twenty-first century, we know many materials more transparent and weaker than Oya stone, and we know that a much more transparent building can be made using glass and acrylic, but Wright's Imperial Hotel evokes strong emotions because of his staunch resolve. He was engaged in a struggle to confront the overwhelming presence of a material.

When I realized this, I knew what to do. I needed to take on materials in the same vein, because the scars of battle stir emotions and move people. Wanting to make architecture weak and make the structure recede into its surroundings was, in effect, a challenge with respect to materials. First, I needed to weaken the materials that I was working with. Still, it is not easy to make materials blend with the environment. They simply do not disappear that easily. This is why a struggle was necessary. The scars resulting from this fight would have meaning that outlives the passing of times. This gave me the courage to use Oya stone, but I wanted to go even further than Wright, forging even deeper scars than he did. Moreover, the holes had to be deep enough not to be considered decorative.

The detail that we used for the Chokkura Plaza and Shelter represented our preempting any such criticism. The holes and disfigurements in the Oya stone were made decisively, with the tectonics of the building in mind. We came up with a new structural system of steel sheets and stone to carve the material. Working as the tensional members, the steel sheets were woven into a diagonal mesh, while the Oya stone, acting as the compression member, was woven into it. In this system, as in a textile, stone is the weft (horizontal thread) and steel is the warp (vertical thread). The openings in this unique fabric make the building appear to merge visually into the surrounding landscape. Although steel and stone are supposed to be tough, robust materials, their rendering as porous structure enables a new flow of space through it.

I realize that my desire to erase architecture is a goal that is impossible to achieve and laden with contradictions. But herein lies the meaning of trying to make architecture disappear. It is brought about by the manifestations of the fight with materials, repeated time and again. Materials only begin to show their true nature when you challenge them at the limits of their capabilities. Even if this fight is as foolish and reckless as that of Don Quixote, the resulting scars will remain as a memento. The fight is a serious one because of its audacity.

When I arrived at this realization, I was released from a problem that had been bothering me for a long time: how to reconcile my intention to make architecture disappear with the necessity of making it iconic. Now I recognize that architecture can also become an icon, when, in the process of trying to erase it from its environment, the architect undertakes the bold task of challenging the overwhelming presence of materials. This is why architecture can become a presence to be remembered. The projects featured in this second monograph were produced after I realized this.

Materiality and Immateriality in the Architecture of Kengo Kuma

—

Botond Bognar

I prefer an ambiguous, unreliable condition, in which the substance is scattered all over the place. I don't want to make particulate architecture but create a particulate condition.…More than, and prior to defining a style, what I desire is to create a certain type of place and a certain type of condition that can be experienced by the human body.

Kengo Kuma, "A Return to Materials"

Committed as much to modernity as to Japanese culture, Kuma, with the best of his completed as well as unbuilt projects, has already set the expectations truly high. Now he is expected to not only continue meeting these in the years to come, but to exceed them.

Botond Bognar, *Kengo Kuma: Selected Works*

At the time of writing my first book on Kuma's work, he was emerging as one of Japan's most promising young architects. It will be the central task of this book to investigate the evolution of his architecture and shed light on how he has fulfilled the promises of earlier work. The answer to the first part of this inquiry is simple; he has achieved a great deal since the publication of his previous monograph. Let me say it here, up front: he has not only met but far surpassed the expectations of those who have continued to observe his career. Today, less than five years since the publication of *Kengo Kuma: Selected Works*, he is one of Japan's most prominent, internationally renowned architects, and for good reason. More prolific and creative than ever, in a few short years he has produced numerous significant projects—with many others on the drawing board—that have attracted the attention and admiration of a wide range of audiences: the public, architects, and critics, as well as clients all over the world. His projects have also won several prestigious awards.[1]

With interest in his work growing, Kuma's architecture is now sought after both in Japan and, perhaps even more so, around the world. More than 50 percent of his commissions come from abroad, and he has branch offices as far away as Beijing and Paris.[2] He is part of the growing internationally active group that can be called, using Esther Charlesworth's term, "architects without frontiers."[3] His work has been extensively published in books, leading journals, and magazines, and exhibited in galleries and museums in Japan, Italy, Germany, Finland, France, Poland, China, the United Kingdom, and the United States, among other places. Moreover, he has been invited to lecture at venues on all continents, and he has held distinguished teaching positions

Kengo Kuma, "A Return to Materials," in Luigi Alini, *Kengo Kuma: Works and Projects* (Milan: Electa Architecture, 2006), 26.

Botond Bognar, *Kengo Kuma: Selected Works* (New York: Princeton Architectural Press, 2005), 41.

1. For the list of Kuma's awards, prizes, and exhibitions, see the Biographical Notes and Awards appendix of this book.

2. Kengo Kuma, conversation with the author, November 2008.

3. Esther Charlesworth, *Architects without Frontiers: War, Reconstruction and Design Responsibility* (Burlington, MA: Architectural Press, 2006).

previous page: **Lotus House, East Japan, 2005**

top left: **Waketokuyama Japanese restaurant, Minato-ku, Tokyo, 2004**

top right: **Nagasaki Prefectural Art Museum, Nagasaki, Nagasaki Prefecture, 2005**

bottom left: **Umbrella Teahouse, I space Gallery, Chicago, Ill., United States, 2008**

bottom right: **Ondo-cho Civic Center, Kure, Hiroshima Prefecture, 2008**

at prominent universities.[4] Among his numerous recent lectures, the one he held at the Royal Academy of Arts in London on July 14, 2008 attracted a huge audience and practically the entire British architecture establishment.

Responding to the second part of the inquiry, how he has been able to achieve so much, takes longer. To reveal the reasons behind Kuma's remarkable success, his current projects must be investigated both in relation to earlier work and in comparison to the work of his contemporaries, especially in Japan, where major transformations have taken place since the economy began to falter some fifteen years ago. Kuma's recent output indicates that his theoretical position and the general direction of his architecture, which he formulated in the early 1990s, have continued to develop and are more elaborate, mature, and impressive today, as underscored by his published essays and books. In addition to being a successful practitioner, Kuma is a prolific writer and has, in recent years, increasingly weighed in on matters of design and architecture.[5]

Along this upward trajectory, his work, now including a wide range of projects from small installations to large urban-scale complexes, is executed with deep conviction and sophistication, more so than before, both at home and abroad. Among his numerous architectural accomplishments, a few representative examples include residential projects such as the Lotus House in the city of Zushi; Yien East/Archipelago in Kyoto; and the Ginzan Onsen Fujiya, a ryokan in the city of Obanazawa in the northern Yamagata Prefecture. Several noteworthy museum commissions include the large Nagasaki Prefectural Art Museum and the Suntory Museum in Tokyo. He has been equally productive and successful in turning out exceptional commercial and community facilities such as the Chokkura Plaza and Shelter in the city of Takanezawa in Tochigi Prefecture; the Z58 Zhongtai Box, an office and showroom building in Shanghai, China; the Ondo Civic Center in the southern Japanese city of Kure; the Asahi Broadcasting Corporation Headquarters in Osaka; and the urban-scale complexes of the Sanlitun Village South and the Sanlitun SOHO, both in Beijing. Adding to this distinguished list, which is by no means exhaustive, are two small but excellent projects: the Japanese restaurants of Waketokuyama in Tokyo and Sake no Hana in London. And just as remarkable are Kuma's growing number of tiny experimental tea pavilions, designed mainly as exhibitions, with unusual materials and innovative techniques. It is clear, even from this short list, that his office is capable of executing just about any size and kind of project with much success.[6]

ARCHITECTURE IN THE POST-BUBBLE ERA

Kuma emerged as part of a generation of architects that launched their careers around the early to mid-1990s, when the high-flying, prosperous, and flamboyantly excessive era of Japan's bubble economy was giving way to one of the longest, and in many respects still ongoing, recessions in the country's history. These economic troubles have also been aggravated by the worsening degradation of the environment, excessive energy consumption and its growing costs, the rapidly aging population and exceedingly low birthrate, the waning of the long-maintained lifetime employment system, and the shift to a globalized information- and service-oriented society. It is not surprising that the new realities of the post-Bubble Era, while setting considerable limitations on construction in the country, ushered in new priorities and created the necessity for a new kind of architecture.[7] Kuma's generation, which includes such noted designers as Jun Aoki (b. 1956), Kazuyo Sejima

4. Kuma held a teaching position at the prestigious Keio University in Tokyo; he is now a professor of architecture at the University of Tokyo, and he follows in the footsteps of such well-known predecessors as Kenzo Tange, Fumihiko Maki, and Tadao Ando. In the 2007–08 academic year, Kuma was appointed Distinguished Endowed Plym Professor at the University of Illinois Urbana-Champaign.

5. For a list of Kuma's most important publications, see the Bibliography appendix of this book.

6. Kengo Kuma and Associates was a relatively small office until 2000, with about fifteen persons working there altogether. Currently, the staff numbers well over seventy and is growing.

7. For additional information on the past twenty-five years in Japanese architecture, see Botond Bognar, *Beyond the Bubble: The New Japanese Architecture* (London: Phaidon Press, 2008) and Thomas Daniell, *After the Crash: Architecture in Post-Bubble Japan* (New York: Princeton Architectural Press, 2008).

(b. 1956), Yoko Kinoshita (b. 1956), Shigeru Ban (b. 1957), Koichi Yasuda (b. 1958), and Hitoshi Abe (b. 1962), faced the challenges of a drastically changed economy and met them by finding new means of creativity through down-to-earth innovations in design.

After the often-difficult start of acquiring commissions and establishing a practice, by the mid-1990s these architects altogether managed to produce a considerably substantial body of work. In their emerging architectures we can recognize a new direction, as they coalesced around a more straightforward and restrained mode of design. This, as in the work of modernist master Ludwig Mies van der Rohe, favors again the idea of "less is more" or the distillation of meaning in architecture, rather than the simple elimination of it. Moreover, compelled to return to the basics, this new generation rediscovered the poetics in the ordinary and the expressive potential of materials, at the same time paying more attention to pressing social and environmental needs. Such priorities are now prefaced with an increasing reliance on the fast progressing digital- and information-based technologies that have been transforming Japanese society and the urban landscape for quite some time.

Needless to say, these new realities pressured the older generation of Japanese designers to change course as well, although some had already been advancing similar, if not identical, modes of minimalist architecture before the bubble burst. These architects adapted to the demands of the new era of far fewer commissions mainly by increasing their work abroad. Fumihiko Maki, Tadao Ando, Yoshio Taniguchi, Toyo Ito, and the firm of Nikken Sekkei remained eminently active on the international contemporary architecture scene, exemplifying this trend.[8] At the same time, many of them shifted the focus of their work toward simpler, less decorative, and, more importantly, green and sustainable architecture. Ando, for instance, has become a staunch environmentalist not just by virtue of his powerful, sensitive, and poetically inspired designs but also as an activist.[9] Nikken Sekkei has been more and more active in recent years in advancing the cause of more effectively ecological architecture by relying on its vast and longstanding experience in energy-saving design and through the application of innovative construction and environmental technologies. Ito, who has shifted strategies several times in his career, is now experimenting with new types of organic architecture that explore materiality and the tectonic dimension of design.

While the architecture of Kuma and his generation shares some tenets in common with that of their more established elders, the two reveal differences as well. Educated in the late 1970s and 1980s, Kuma's generation had no direct involvement in Japan's previous architectural movements, instigated by the nearly limitless possibilities of the chaotic bubble years. This was a time when commercialism in overdrive ruled the practice of architecture, and in which the striking form or seductive image of a building was valued above all. Likewise, this new generation of architects did not experience the nation's earlier trademark movement, Metabolism, which dominated the 1960s and early 1970s. Kuma and his peers were not indoctrinated with a fetish for the megastructural systems and industrial technologies from which the Metabolist architects derived their theories and designs. Yet, unlike the first generation of post-Metabolist architects—who, disillusioned by the destructive side of unrestrained technological progress, rejected the notion of high technology as being the salvation for architecture—Kuma's generation did not shy away from either the expressive potential of tectonics or the benefits of integrating technology into architecture. Nevertheless, they had to find their

8. Postwar Japanese architects are considered to comprise some five generations to date. The first one included Kenzo Tange, Kunio Maekawa, and Junzo Sakakura; the second, Fumihiko Maki, Arata Isozaki, Kisho Kurokawa, and Kazuo Shinohara; the third, Tadao Ando, Toyo Ito, and Itsuko Hasegawa; the fourth, Kazuyo Sejima, Jun Aoki, Shigeru Ban, and Kengo Kuma; while the just-now-emerging fifth generation would include Atelier Bow-Wow, Shuhei Endo, Tezuka Architects, Tele-design, and Makoto Takei and Chie Nabeshima Architects (TNA).

9. Ando has initiated and actively promoted several programs to plant thousands of trees in areas devastated by natural disasters or other causes. He launched the first such campaign after the 1995 Great Hyogo Earthquake that destroyed much of the city of Kobe.

top: **Tadao Ando: Awaji Yumebutai, Awaji Island,**
Japan, 2000

bottom left: **Toyo Ito: Meiso no Mori Funeral Hall, Kakamigahara,**
Japan, 2004

bottom right: **Shigeru Ban: Glass Shutter House, Tokyo, 2003**

own way of grounding their designs in a rapidly changing economy and a culture in which conditions have, since the mid-1990s, been austere and challenging.

Kuma's maturation as an architect was nevertheless somewhat different from that of others in his generation, many of whom are now returning to minimalism and reiterating some of architecture's high-modern tenets in refreshing ways. Kuma's ideas and his understanding of architecture have been shaped by diverse experiences and influences, with varying intensities and in unique combinations. The first of these, as he often recollects, was the traditional wooden house in Yokohama where he lived as a child, with its deep, shadowy interiors. When he was ten years old, the newly constructed 1964 Tokyo Olympic Gymnasium, designed by Kenzo Tange, amazed him and also played a role in his decision to become an architect.[10] In the late 1970s, he studied under Hiroshi Hara at Tokyo University, and his mentor's interest in vernacular buildings drew his attention toward an area of study that, at the time, was not a source of inspiration for most architects. He might also have been attracted to the "floating world" of Hara's idiosyncratic designs, in which reality and illusion blended seamlessly.[11] Yet Kuma also differed from his mentor; unlike Hara, he favored a less decorative interpretation of traditional architecture, which included representative examples of native African architecture in addition to Japanese.[12]

His appreciation for spatial layering and simplicity of design elements may have been influenced by another teacher of his at Tokyo University, Fumihiko Maki.[13] Maki's designs are characterized by the application of modernist architectural elements but with a rather free-spirited or nonmodernist manner of combining them into larger entities, often as layered collages, within both architectural and urban projects. The spatial design of Maki's large urban-scale work reflects his sympathy for the flexible organization of premodern or vernacular settlements, and some of Kuma's recent urban complexes reveal features not unlike the ones favored by Maki.[14] Since the two designers shared similar preferences, Maki persuaded Kuma to continue his studies and assisted him in going to Columbia University, where in 1985, with the help of a Fulbright Fellowship, he became a visiting researcher. Here, in addition to learning about American architecture, he delved into the lessons of Asian urbanism.

Kuma's interest in architectural traditions and their contemporary relevance was further reinforced in 1991, when he received the commission for Water/Glass, a guesthouse in Atami, a city in Shizuoka Prefecture. The site of the building is adjacent to Bruno Taut's only extant work in Japan, the Hyuga Villa (1936).[15] When Kuma visited the villa, the aspect that impressed him most was not how skillfully Taut had applied traditional elements such as tatami mats and sliding panels of shoji and fusuma, but, rather, his splendid appropriation of an intense but intimate relationship between the traditional Japanese house and nature. One might say that these experiences were, for Kuma, an architectural rediscovery of Taut; in his childhood, he had already encountered the work of this early-modern German architect. Kuma's father, an art lover, was very fond of Taut's designs and had collected several of his small artifacts: wooden cups, boxes, and utensils. This occurrence in Kuma's life is important, because it reveals that he, like many Japanese architects, came to appreciate traditional architecture, at least partially, through the influence of foreigners like Taut and Wright, who admired and learned from Japanese traditions, implementing them within their work.

10. Kuma refers to these experiences in "A Return to Materials," in Luigi Alini, *Kengo Kuma: Works and Projects* (Milan: Electa Architecture, 2006), 26.

11. "Floating world" is a reference to Edo-period urban lifestyles and architecture, which cherished a world of earthly pleasures and an easygoing and somewhat decadent outlook on life.

12. Kuma traveled extensively throughout Africa as a member of Hara's university research group in 1979.

13. Maki is well known for his research and theories of urban design, one of which is his *Investigations in Collective Form* (St. Louis, MO: Washington University Press, 1964).

14. Like Hara in the 1970s, Maki was also interested in the spatial organization of indigenous settlements. With the support of a Graham Foundation Fellowship, he traveled extensively in Africa, the Mediterranean, and Asia to investigate the native architecture of these cultures.

15. Escaping from Nazi Germany, Taut came to Japan in 1933. He summarized his experience of traditional Japanese architecture and his admiration of it in several books and essays. He built two houses in Japan; only the Atami Hyuga Villa on the Izu Peninsula has survived.

top: **Kenzo Tange: Olympic Gymnasium,**
Tokyo, Japan, 1964

middle left: **Fumihiko Maki: Spiral Building,**
Tokyo, Japan, 1985

middle right: **Hiroshi Hara: Yukian Tea**
House, Ikaho, Japan, 1988

bottom: **Water/Glass, Atami, Shizuoka**
Prefecture, 1995

top: **Cityscape of Shibuya, Tokyo, as a "dream machine," in August 1991**

middle left: **Shin Takamatsu: Kirin Plaza Building, Osaka, Japan, 1987**

middle right: **Kazuo Shinohara: Tokyo Institute of Technology, Centennial Hall, Tokyo, Japan, 1987**

left: **Tadao Ando: Water Temple, Awaji Island, Hyogo Prefecture, Japan, 1991**

After returning home from New York during the dizzyingly frantic era of urban development that characterized the Bubble Era of the late 1980s, Kuma came under the spell of the Japanese city, especially Tokyo. The city's chaotic and particularly non-Western qualities—its vitality, resilience, spatial flexibility, and friendly neighborhood communities—were by this time rediscovered and appreciated as never before, by architects, urbanists, and the public alike. Between the 1950s and mid-1970s, when the principles and aesthetic standards of modernism dominated Japanese culture, antagonism toward the Japanese city was strong. To the chagrin of modernists, Tokyo has a fragmentary and heterogeneous disposition. It lacks clear organization and public monuments, and does not have an "old city" core or open public center. Yet it is impressively dynamic and, with all of the latest fashionable attractions of a desirable "dream machine," futuristic. After the age of modernism, growing admiration for Tokyo meant that the city itself had become a model for its architecture as well, and architects eagerly appropriated its nonmodernist qualities into their designs. Such developments, brought about by Bubble Era conditions, also signified the epitome of postmodernism in Japanese architecture.

It is important, however, to emphasize that postmodernism in Japan is different from its counterpart in Europe, and especially in the United States. While image-driven in general and often decorative—like many works of Shin Takamatsu, Atsushi Kitagawara, and even Arata Isozaki—Japanese postmodern architecture rarely ventured into the formalistic, literal, and sentimental appropriation of classicist styles. It was, above all, derivative of and a commentary on the attributes of urban culture and the contemporary Japanese city. The huge architectural output produced between the mid-1980s and mid-1990s reveals various instances of enthusiastic, ironic, enigmatic, and truly thoughtful responses, but it also included many opportunistic and nonsensical reactions to the volatile urban environments of Japan. Indeed, the vast riches of the Bubble Era economy and its often recklessly adventurous mentality encouraged and funded all of these projects, and while the majority were inferior and tasteless "designs," they produced a large number of exceptional works of world-class architecture, such as Ando's Water Temple in Hyogo Prefecture. Representing the broad international recognition of these achievements, *Time* magazine and other publications referred to this as the Golden Age of Japanese design.[16]

THE EARLY STAGES OF KUMA'S ARCHITECTURE

It was around this time, in the late 1980s, when Kuma launched his architectural practice and began to formulate his ideas about design. He established his small atelier, Spatial Design Studio, in partnership with Satoko Shinohara in Tokyo in 1987. The first project that the partnership produced, the Small Bath House in Izu (1988), was a rather simple and pleasant wooden structure with a design that featured an unmistakably fragmentary composition, adding one more to the many already mushrooming in Japan around that time. Kuma later explained his design strategy, which in this project was still more intuitive than rational: "I already knew I wanted to break up architecture into particles when I designed my first architectural work...but I had not yet put that desire into words. All I wanted to do was to fragment architecture."[17]

Kuma began speculating about the nature of the relationship between architecture and context when he first started to work in the urban environment, after setting up his own office, Kengo Kuma and Associates, in Tokyo in

16. "Japanese Design: The Golden Age," *Time*, September 21, 1987, cover story.

17. Kengo Kuma, "Particle on Horizontal Plane," *Japan Architect* 38 (Summer 2000): 120.

1990. Interpreting the Japanese city, and Tokyo in particular, as a built fabric characterized by a fragmentary and chaotic disposition, he conceived of subsequent projects in this manner and, in doing so, integrated his architecture into the city. The fragments from which he assembled his first few projects were, however, borrowed from the architectural vocabulary of classicism, somewhat in the vein of Robert Venturi and Denise Scott Brown. Built in 1991 and made of concrete, the M2, Rustic, and Doric buildings in Tokyo were heavy, large, monumental, explicitly classical, and even decorative. In short, these buildings carried just about all the hallmarks that Kuma would eventually fiercely reject in subsequent work. Admitting his miscalculations, he wrote, "When I designed the M2 Building...I believed that if I created an architecture of fragmentation, the building would dissolve and blend into the chaos that surrounded it.[18] Elsewhere he was more explicitly self-critical: "There was something wrongheaded about first creating an object and then trying to make it disappear. The problem...was in thinking that design necessarily meant the design and creation of objects."[19] Clearly, after such mistakes, Kuma needed to change his modus operandi.

The break came in 1991 with a new commission for the Kiro-san Observatory on Yoshiumi Island in the Inland Sea, which gave him the opportunity to rethink his initial strategy of trying to blend an architectural object into its environment by fragmenting its form into a largely random collection of classical elements. Here, Kuma wanted a design that would preserve the natural landscape. He came to the solution of cutting a void, like a deep crevice, into the mountaintop with only two thin platforms sticking out from it, rather than placing a towerlike structure on a bulldozed peak. In practical terms, this was an act of burying or covering up architecture. Through this process, Kuma's now well-known credo was slowly crystallizing: "I want to erase architecture. I have always wanted to do so, and I am not likely to change my mind."[20]

Needless to say, such a statement from an architect about to start his career in earnest, without explanation, seems utterly paradoxical. Even for Kuma, the realization of this intention, in practical terms, left much to think about. It resulted in various interpretations of the notion, as well as extensive and strategic experimentations during the years to come. It is evident that burying architecture underground, as in the case of the Kiro-san Observatory, closely approximates the act of erasure. As there are no exterior volumes or elevations to look at, the experience of a buried building is limited to the interiors and, in this case, also to the views of the spectacular outside landscape and the Inland Sea. Kuma repeated the same strategy in a later project, the Kitakami Canal Museum, where he buried the small facility in the embankment of the Kitakami River. He also proposed underground solutions in some of his early competition entries, such as the Japan Museum in Tokyo and the Kansai-kan of the National Diet Library located south of Kyoto, neither of which he won. Indeed, the problem with the strategy of burying architecture underground is that its actual application is rare, sometimes impractical, and often unacceptable by the client.[21]

The issue for Kuma was then to explore other options that may be available for him to "erase" architecture. The Kiro-san Observatory taught him a very important lesson: architecture could be made to "disappear" if it had no exterior. Theoretically, the condition of erasure could be attained if the object quality of a building, what we usually confront as outsiders, could be effectively neutralized so that the experiencing person could always feel like an

18. Kengo Kuma, "Introduction," in Botond Bognar, *Kengo Kuma: Selected Works* (New York: Princeton Architectural Press, 2005), 14.

19. Kengo Kuma, "Digital Gardening," *Space Design*, November 1997, 6.

20. Kuma does not recall precisely when he first made this statement; it occurred to him around 1991, when he was designing the Kiro-san Observatory. According to my review of his published documents, it first appeared in printed form in 1997, in his essay "Digital Gardening," ibid.

21. We now know from Kuma himself that it was the perceived disappearance of architecture that prevented several of his entries from winning competitions, as the clients wanted to have an architecture that could stand up as a visible and memorable symbol. See Kuma's Introduction (p. 8). Yet, within the growing trend of ecological design and its increased care for the natural environment, many architects, such as Ando, Ito, Nikken Sekkei, have designed projects at least partially underground.

top: **M2 Building, Tokyo, Japan, 1988**

middle: **Kiro-san Observatory, Yoshiumi Island, 1994**

left: **Kitakami Canal Museum, Ishinomaki, Miyagi Prefecture, 1999**

insider within its environment. Kuma found an analogy that could illustrate his idea, and perhaps guide his design as well, in gardening. In his seminal essay "Digital Gardening," he stated, "Architecture must be planned as a frame for viewing the environment from within."[22] Then he continued with the following explanation:

> The practice of gardening provides us with many hints and gives us courage. Gardening and landscape planning deal with the same domain but are different disciplines. That is the key point. As the 'scape' in landscape indicates, landscape planning is a scenic art and a visual methodology. The planner stands 'outside' the landscape and visually manipulates it. In gardening, on the other hand, no privileged position from which a 'planner' observes and manipulates the scenery exists. The 'gardener' is always inside the garden.[23]

Very importantly, Kuma does not consider vision as primary in kindling the feeling of being an insider in an environment. He recognizes that the gardener, while seeing the garden always from within, is not merely an observer. The gardener is the caretaker and, as such, the one who cultivates the garden and actively participates in its creation, and whose experiences or perceptions of being an insider are intimately tied to those activities.

Kuma's theories about gardening, designing, or cultivating architecture as an environment reveal many aspects that are closely related to the essence of traditional Japanese residential architecture. This is not surprising, because he arrived at these realizations after a visit to Taut's Hyuga Villa drew his attention to the timelessness of this architecture.[24] Traditionally, the Japanese house has been conceived not as a monumental or dominant center or as an object within its environment, be it urban or natural, but as an integral part of it. Kuma was prompted to recognize the flexible or ambiguous spatial organization of the house, the indeterminate or variable disposition of its boundaries, and its intensive relationship to the garden or larger surrounding environment. In many respects, the Japanese house was created as an extension of nature, and so was regarded as a form of nature transformed by and existing within nature. The use of natural and often untreated materials reinforced the occupants' sense that they still lived within nature.

In early 1992, Kuma started work on the Water/Glass residence in Atami.[25] The commission called for a small but elegant guesthouse on a steep hillside with spectacular views of the sea below. He employed several strategies to prevent the visitor from encountering the building as an outsider. From where the house is entered at the street, he designed only a blank wall, like a high fence with a wide sliding gate. Through it, the visitor immediately enters the spatial matrix of the building's interior, which has a porous quality, because it is penetrated by an intricate system of open passages and light courts. The steep location also helped Kuma in his efforts not to reveal the building from the outside. Perched on a ledge, the very narrow site does not allow people to go around the house, and thus its exterior cannot be experienced from any other direction. If an outside view is possible at all, it would be only from miles away, from which distance every individual building would "disappear" anyway.

Having thus achieved a "neutralization" of the exterior, he then concentrated on the interior, opening spaces to outside views as much as possible by eliminating solid exterior walls. He used intermediary zones

22. Kuma, "Digital Gardening," 7.

23. Ibid., 8.

24. Taut visited the Katsura Villa a few days after he arrived in Japan in 1933, and praised it as a forerunner of modern architecture. His writings in this regard rediscovered and reintroduced the villa as an exceptional example of traditional Japanese architecture. See Bruno Taut, *Houses and People of Japan*, trans. Estille Balk (London: John Gifford, 1938).

25. In many of his early works, Kuma selected dual names to indicate the major theme of the architecture; these include River/Filter (1996), Ocean/City (1997), Water/Slats (1998), Sea/Filter (2001), and Forest/Floor (2003).

top left and right: **Katsura Imperial Villa, Kyoto, Japan, seventeenth century**

left and bottom: **Water/Glass, Atami, Shizuoka Prefecture, 1995**

to mediate between inside and outside. On the first floor, he surrounded the large hall with glass-enclosed verandas, and over part of the second floor he designed a wide-open terrace covered entirely with a reflective pool beneath the roof's overhanging multilayered glass eaves. Floating on this pool of water is an all-glass oval-shaped lounge, where the horizontal floor plate of frosted glass seems to be the only firm indication of the boundaries of the space. At the same time, the surface of the pool, with its overflowing edges forming an artificial horizon, extends the presence of the water toward views of the ocean in the far distance below. The experience is not unlike the one brought about by the strategy of *shakkei* (borrowed scenery that Japanese garden designers used to great advantage in the past to create illusive expansions of often very small gardens). Inspired by his experiences of the Hyuga Villa, this guesthouse was also as much an act of homage to Taut as it was to traditional Japanese architecture, without any literal iteration of them.

The spectacular Water/Glass residence is also the first project in which Kuma used a system of stainless-steel louvers placed under the glass roof to break up light into vibrant particles and bounce it onto the surface of the lounge's water and glass floor. He discovered that densely spaced louvers can both transmit and reflect light and, in doing so, render a vibrant mirage. In this case, his love for and response to the presence of the ocean shifted his own understanding of architecture and launched a series of new design strategies. In "The Ocean Changed My Architecture," Kuma wrote, by introducing "louvers derived from the waters....the ocean provided the concept of the particles."[26] Indeed, while his overall goal of erasing architecture remained the same, its intended realization was to change according to the type of building, location, and other circumstances. Kuma, as he said, tries "to listen as carefully as possible to the site."[27]

"PARTICLIZATION" AND THE BLURRING OF ARCHITECTURE

The completion of his much-acclaimed Water/Glass residence in 1995 brought an increase in commissions. Although the traditional idea of defining spaces primarily through horizontal surfaces such as thin floor plates, canopies, or roofs has remained a significant feature of Kuma's architecture—as in the Forest/Floor, the Horai Onsen Bath House, and more recently his Glass House in New Canaan, Connecticut—he has also introduced new elements and strategies. Among these, foremost is an extensive use of slats to demarcate architectural boundaries. It might be said that, in such instances, he turned previous applications of horizontal louvers into vertical systems of spatial filters. At the Noh Stage in the Forest and at his River/Filter Japanese noodle restaurant in Tamakawa, Fukushima Prefecture, louvers were made into curtainlike wooden screens, and they were suspended vertically in front of the main facades for privacy and sun protection. In both instances, the use of louverlike screens is still only partial, but they contribute to a softer appearance of surfaces and thus the ambiguous disposition of architecture.

In several subsequent projects, such as Wood/Slats guesthouse in Kanagawa Prefecture, the Ando Hiroshige Museum in Bato-machi, and the recently built House in Aoyama in Tokyo, the application of densely spaced slats is so predominant that just about every part of these buildings becomes completely defined by these infinitely repeated elements. This happens, first of all, along the outside boundaries, such as facades and roofs, but also frequently with interior partitions. With this new mode of design, Kuma arrived

26. Kengo Kuma, "The Ocean Changed My Architecture," in *Kengo Kuma: Materials, Structures and Details* (Basel: Birkhäuser, 2004), 71–72.

27. **Kengo Kuma and** Hiroyuki Suzuki, "A Return to Materials," *Japan Architect* 38 (Summer 2000): 4.

top: **Horai Onsen Bath House, Atami, Shizuoka Prefecture, Japan, 2003**

middle: **River/Filter noodle restaurant, Tamakawa, Fukushima Prefecture, 1996**

bottom left and right: **Ando Hiroshige Museum, Bato-machi, 2000**

top left: **House in Aoyama, Tokyo, 2009**

top right: **JR Shibuya Station, facade renovation, Shibuya-ku, Tokyo, 2003**

bottom left: **Ando Hiroshige Museum, Bato-machi, Tochigi Prefecture, 2000**

bottom right: **Cocon Karasuma, Nakagyo-ku, Kyoto, 2005**

at another major stage in his architecture, even though he had already been promoting the particlization of architecture and, even further, its broader environment, for quite a while.

For him, particlization meant undermining the monolithic objectlike appearance of a building and rendering it less definitive or solid so that it becomes permeable, ephemeral, and appears to have less bodily substance, almost as if it were a phenomenon. In Kuma's words:

> I want to create a condition that is as vague and ambiguous as drifting particles. The closest thing to such a condition is a rainbow. A rainbow is not an actual object, and that is what makes it attractive.[28]

More contemporary analogies such as pixelation or digitization are appropriate descriptions of the resulting effect; Kuma's facades and surfaces are also reminiscent of bar codes.[29] In either case, the result of particlization is not unlike the effects of digital renderings. The appearance of his slatted buildings is comparable to low-resolution prints or photos that are out of focus or in the process of fading. In effect, he presents us with a kind of fragile architecture that seems as if it might dissipate like clouds or else fade into the environment.

These issues necessitate a return to his ideas about digital gardening, because the term *digital*, although an overt reference to his theory of parti-clization and his pixelation of materials, directly denotes his application of actual digital technologies. Along with other electrographic displays, digital images have been instrumental for Kuma in dissolving the distinction between the real and the fictive—in other words, in blurring architecture. In a 1997 pro-posal for a memorial park to be dedicated to the late employees of a private company in Gumma Prefecture, for example, he combined the natural land-scape with high technology. In a sunken gardenlike space, the names of the deceased were etched into large glass panes. After finding the proper person, visitors could make contact with and recall the deceased with the help of computers and monitor screens, by viewing video images and listening to their voices.

Another, perhaps more telling, example of digitization is his facade renovation of the JR Shibuya Station in Tokyo, where he installed three sheets of glass printed with low-resolution digital images of clouds, placed one-quarter inch apart, creating a moiré effect in which the shapes and colors of the clouds changed continuously according to the observer's movement. As real clouds are reflected on the same glass surface, they blend with the photographs. In this project, Kuma succeeded remarkably in not only erasing the architecture but also in dissolving the distinction between the real and the virtual. Kuma employed a similar layering in his renovation of a 1938 building in Kyoto for the facade of Cocon Karasuma, which is composed of transparent, colorfully patterned glass panels applied over the old building, both covering and revealing the preexisting architecture. Visual ambiguity is also a promi-nent quality of spatial perception inside the Ando Hiroshige Museum, where numerous reflective glass walls simultaneously generate both transparencies and mirrored images.

The most striking example of Kuma's digital gardening, however, is an unrealized competition project for a museum dedicated to the work of the late Nam June Paik, the internationally renowned Korean multimedia artist. The one-level complex stretches horizontally through a narrow and shallow

28. Kuma, "Dissolution of the Object and Flight from the City," *Japan Architect* 38 (Summer 2000): 58.

29. Greg Lynn has likened Kuma's architecture of slats to pointillism or pixelation in the paintings of the well-known French painters Georges Seurat (1859–1891) and Paul Signac (1863–1935). Greg Lynn, "Pointillism," *Space Design* November 1997, 46.

wooded valley and appropriates the sloping and undulating terrain as its floor. This indoor garden was to be covered with a multilayer glass roof, with a steel structure sandwiched between the glass layers. Flooded with a thin sheet of water that cascades down at the lower edge of the roof, the entire space beneath it becomes enveloped in water. Between the horizontal layers of glass, Kuma arranged, in the pattern of a rectangular grid, hundreds of active computer monitors facing up from under the water. In such a display, the live monitors would add up to a large pixelated surface on which visitors could walk. Once again, by means of the reflective pool on glass and the digital images on the screens, Kuma elicited a human experience of ambiguity, which can be compared to many works of his early mentor Hara. For example, in his Kenju Park Forest House of 1987, Hara carefully arranged numerous glass surfaces in a zigzag pattern with intricately reflected images that opened up a field of perception in which visual reality was effectively rendered indefinite. As the continuation of its surrounding nature, the exterior disappears, limiting the experience of architecture mainly to the interior.

MINIMALISM AND MATERIALITY

Kuma's strategy of digitization, or particlization, is an interesting contrast to his initial design methodology of fragmenting architectural form, which paradoxically led to his explicitly formalistic early architecture. In his design approach developed since the early 1990s, he fragments surfaces as well as materials, while making architectural forms as simple or neutral as possible. In other words, his designs today reveal a curious tendency to remain anonymous in that his approach is a clear rejection of the flamboyant, excessively decorative, and heavily formalistic signature designs that characterized most, if not all, of the buildings constructed in the Bubble Era of the 1980s and early 1990s; it also testifies to his refusal to participate in the now widespread trend of producing twisted, contorted, and seductive but largely empty or meaningless architecture. Addressing this problem, historian William Curtis recently wrote that "architecture today is in danger of degenerating into a game played with over-complicated forms and computer generated images…[which reveal] an obsession with willful imagery, excessive visual rhetoric and vapid form-making for its own sake."[30] The Finnish theoretician and critic Juhani Pallasmaa, writing about Kuma's work, put it this way:

> Today's architectural world is obsessed with the uniqueness of form, immediately identifiable as the hand of its designer. In our age of consumerism and the seductive visual image, buildings are judged by their power to surprise and provoke rather than their capacity to make sense of the human existential reality. Aspirations for universality and anonymity have been discarded, and these objectives are regarded as signs of artistic conservatism….Kengo Kuma is an architect who aims at a distinct quietness, a disciplined understatement in his architectural expression, and the disengagement of his architect's persona.[31]

Kuma's intentions and quality of work reflect the more limited economic climate of Post-Bubble Japan, where today there are other initiatives to promote similarly prudent and anonymous kinds of design. One example is the retail company Muji, which designs and sells its own growing number of brandless household and consumer goods. Muji's impressive yet inexpensive products are characterized by a no-frills minimalist aesthetic that favors

30. William Curtis, on the poster of a public lecture entitled "Gestures Without Meaning: The Crisis of the Star-system," delivered at the University of Illinois Study Abroad Program in Versailles, France, on April 7, 2008.

31. Juhani Pallasmaa, "Veils of Light: Kengo Kuma's Filters of Perception," in Kevin Erickson, *Kengo Kuma: 2007–2008 Plym Distinguished Professor, School of Architecture University of Illinois at Urbana-Champaign* (Urbana, IL: School of Architecture, University of Illinois, 2008), 21.

top: **Hiroshi Hara: Kenju Park Forest Park,
Nakaniida, Japan, 1987**

left: **Nam June Paik Museum, South Korea,
unbuilt, 1997**

simplicity, functionality, and ecological production, as well as a no-brand marketing policy. The name is short for *mujirushi ryóhin*, which actually means "no brand quality goods." The internationally renowned graphic designers Ikko Tanaka and Kenya Hara, along with interior designer Takashi Sugimoto, established the company in the early 1980s with the intention of blending traditional Japanese aesthetics with high-quality modern design.[32] Kuma has worked with members of Muji on several occasions. One of the most important results of this collaboration is Muji House, a prototype prefabricated residence.[33]

Kuma's architecture is indeed minimalist, and it has features in common with the work of his peers, who share his design predilection; however, it also differs in many respects. For example, Kazuyo Sejima and SANAA's increasingly severe minimalism, which often results in hardly more than built architectural diagrams with no articulated details, can be contrasted with Kuma's work, which is restrained and serene yet rich in textures, colors, and intricately modulated light.[34] More than anything, he unfailingly concentrates on the totality of human experience, which involves not only vision but all faculties of perception, especially tactility and movement. Underlying these efforts is his recognition that architecture by definition is a structure, a material entity that needs to withstand a variety of environmental forces and impacts, and this material condition has to be reckoned with when trying to render it a phenomenon, or mirage. Therefore, the issue of materiality had to become more and more part of the picture, prompting him to deal with it rather early, and increasingly later on, in a wide variety of ways depending on the nature of the material.

A growing interest in materiality is evident today not only in Kuma's work but also in that of many other Japanese architects. In general, rather than pursuing the formalistic, not to mention decorative, solutions that characterized so much architecture in the 1980s and beyond, Japanese architects are now more interested in exploring the potentials of new and old materials. This, of course, does not mean that materials did not play an important role in Bubble Era architecture; however, during those times architects were more inclined to use them as architectural finishes, such as aluminum or stainless-steel plates and stone veneer, which masked rather than revealed the tectonic structure underneath. Today, the younger generation architects have an especially different take on materials; more often, they use them as naked elements or structures, as a way to shape innovative architectures. Kuma puts it this way:

> The conclusion I have reached after having thought about materials in various forms is simple. Material is not a finish. Period....What is important is that we distance ourselves from the twofold division of structures...and materials....The term "Material Structure," which I coined...threads together material and structure into one.[35]

This point is well illustrated by his remarkable Great Bamboo Wall, a mall guesthouse north of Beijing, where he used bamboo extensively to define the boundaries of the building and the interior of a tea pavilion. As in previous economic recessions in the early and late 1970s, today's interest in innovative uses of materials is also fostered by the Post-Bubble times, characterized by more stringent requirements, greater restraint, and more economically and ecologically favorable solutions.

32. Ikko Tanaka, born in Nara, Japan, in 1930, is also a tea master. Takashi Sugimoto, born in Tokyo in 1945, runs his own interior design office, the well-noted Super Potato Design in Tokyo. Kenya Hara, born in 1958, the director of Muji since 2001, leads his Nippon Design Center in Tokyo and teaches at the Musashino Art University; one of his interests is the traditional Japanese aesthetic and philosophical notion of emptiness or *mu*. He aims at designing circumstances or conditions, rather than things.

33. In Kuma's Muji House , called *Mado-no-le* (Window House), windows can be freely positioned to suit the owner's aesthetic preference. The project won a Good Design Award in 2008 from the Japan Industrial Design Promotion Organization. It was exhibited alongside seventy other winners in the Tokyo Midtown Design Hub.

34. SANAA stands for "Sejima And Nishizawa Architects Associates," the office of the partnership of Kazuyo Sejima and Ryue Nishizawa.

35. Kengo Kuma, "Material is Not a Finish," in *Kengo Kuma: Materials, Structures and Details* (Basel: Birkhäuser, 2004), 9.

top: **Mado-no-Ie, the Muji House,**
prototype, 2009

middle and bottom: **Great Bamboo Wall,**
tea pavilion, north of Beijing, China, 2002

This general trend is well illustrated by the practices of such architects as Ban, who has been using cardboard and paper tubes in many of his works, as well as Shuhei Endo, who specializes in the application of readily available corrugated metal products. The use of steel-plate or Cor-ten steel in architectural construction is also increasing and can be seen in such projects as Sejima's House in a Plum Tree Grove and Toyo Ito's Mikimoto Ginza, both in Tokyo, and Tezuka Architects' Matsunoyama Science Museum in rural northern Japan, where the entire complex is constructed of Cor-ten steel plates as a solution for sustaining the weight and lateral pressure of the more than twelve feet (four meters) of snow that falls there annually. Ando's architecture has also shifted; he designed two of his recent projects, the hhstyle.com/casa and the gallery 21_21 Design Sight in Tokyo, using large steel plates. And, of course, with the number of new glass products growing, there is a revival of glass architecture, and no one is more eager to explore the use of this material than SANAA. Some of the firm's buildings, such as the Glass Pavilion at the Toledo Museum of Art in Toledo, Ohio, are constructed almost entirely of glass.

Kuma's approach to materials is, in many respects, at variance with those of his peers. No one has been experimenting with materials as diverse as he has; more importantly, no one has applied them in so many different ways. He is attracted, most of all, to natural materials but has not shied away from artificial ones like glass-fiber-reinforced plastic, shape-memory alloy metals, ceramics, Teflon-coated fabric, thick vinyl sheets, and others. Among the natural, old, and time-proven materials, wood is a favorite of his. He also frequently applies bamboo, adobe, paper, ivy and other plants, dry reed, and stone to his architecture. A particularly innovative use of stone appears in the LVMH Shinsaibashi building in Osaka, where the facade is composed of panels of 0.16-inch thick (four-millimeter) translucent onyx sheets from Pakistan, sandwiched between glass plates, alternating with panels of stone-patterned film applied between layers of glass. A similar solution is seen inside his Tiffany Ginza building in Tokyo; however, the textured stone placed between the glass sheets in this case is from China. Earth, water, and light, both natural and artificial, are equally important "materials" for him, as he feels strong devotion to them.

Kuma often juxtaposes old and new materials as a means to conjure unexpected meanings for both, an effect that is best exemplified in his tea pavilions. In general, he is determined to avoid treating these materials as solid masses, bulky volumes, or large components. Regardless of the material, he makes every effort to break it down to small elements or particles; for example, some partitions in his Nasu History Museum are woven of dried vines. This is already visible in many of his earlier works, such as the Stone Plaza, where 1.56-inch-thin (four-centimeter) and 5-feet-long (1.5-meter) stone bars provide a system of horizontal louvers, or the Plastic House, where slim fiber-reinforced plastic rods, measuring one by two inches (2.3 by five centimeters) in section, create both vertical and horizontal screens. Similarly good examples are the already discussed Ando Hiroshige Museum and Masanari Murai Museum. His exploration of materials has continued with even more determination, skill, and artistry in recent works. Take, for example, the Lotus House in Zushi, where a lacy stone curtain creates the outside boundary of the house.

With respect to his use of stone, the solid and unaccommodating quality of the material was initially discomforting to him. In 1996, however, he received a commission to design the Stone Plaza and Museum, a small

top left: **LVMH, translucent onyx stone and glass facade, detail at daytime, Osaka, 2004**

top right: **Tiffany Ginza, interior detail of textured stone in glass, Tokyo, 2008**

bottom left: **Nasu History Museum, detail of woven vines, Nasu-Gun, Tochigi Prefecture, 2000**

bottom right: **Plastic House, fiber-reinforced plastic rods, Tokyo, 2008**

building displaying various stone artifacts. His client, Nobuo Shirai, the owner and manager of a nearby stone-cutting business, wanted a building constructed out of stone from his quarry. This was the same stone that two preexisting storehouses on the site had been constructed out of. After some hesitation and negotiations, Kuma accepted the request. Relying on the help and mastery of Shirai, he was able to experiment and eventually cut the stone into thin bars, which he used horizontally, similar to louvers, as a porous enclosure for the building. The design and completion of this project was a difficult four-year-long process but also a major accomplishment in Kuma's efforts to overcome the resistance of this hard and unyielding material. Yet the real challenge came when he started working on the Chokkura Plaza and Shelter in Takenazawa.[36] His goal was to apply the same kind of stone used in a small preexisting storehouse on the site, a structure that he intended to keep after renovating it. Again, he was determined to make the boundaries of the new building as permeable as possible, like a lacy textile or veil with as many openings or gaps as material, perhaps even more. Difficulty arose from the fact that the stone used in the storehouse was Oya stone, a soft and weak material. He had no choice but to use it in combination with steel sheets arranged in a diagonal mesh. In this hybrid structure, stone acts as the horizontal or compression layer, while the steel functions as the vertical or tension layer, giving the walls a truly vibrant texture.

In the Lotus House, Kuma went a step further. He suspended small, thin travertine plates in a checkerboard pattern from the house's eaves by means of flexible chains of flat-bar steel, which he then anchored to the ground. The screen is not only permeable but also pliable, and it sways gently in the wind. In the Ginzan Onsen Fujiya, he took the application of bamboo to a new territory. Previously, he used bamboo as found in nature, with its cylindrical structure intact. In this ryokan, however, the bamboo was sliced into almost unimaginably thin, 0.16-inch (four-millimeter) strips. Roughly 1.2 million of these strips were attached to the wooden structural frame of the building to form delicately fragile screens. In the case of the Fukuzaki Hanging Garden, thick and soft overlapping vinyl sheets were used to create the entire front facade and most of the interior partitions of a temporary indoor playground. A growing number of small teahouse projects has also given him opportunities to experiment with unusual materials and structures. One example is the traveling installation the Oribe Teahouse, which uses small slices of corrugated plastic arranged in layers and spaced 2.5 inches (six centimeter) apart for both the structure and enclosure.

There is one material that Kuma cannot come to terms with. He has a strong antipathy toward concrete, especially the poured-in-place kind. He has admitted this frequently, and in his "A Return to Materials," he wrote:

> Of course…concrete [can look] fairly attractive, but my other senses, accustomed to the house in which I had grown up, [are] unable to adapt to the idea of the raw concrete box.…Perhaps it is no exaggeration to say that…my professional career has been focused on a single goal: escaping the clutches of concrete.[37]

He finds naked or unfinished concrete too massive, monolithic, and monumental to be suitable for human comfort. This preference provides an interesting difference between the work of Kuma and that of Ando, who designs in heavy, unfinished concrete. While both have great reverence

36. See Kuma's Introduction (p.10).

37. Kuma and Suzuki, "A Return to Materials," in Alini, *Kengo Kuma*, 15.

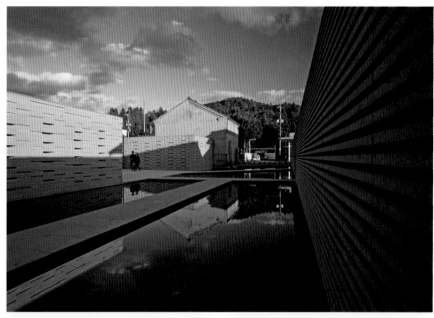

top left: **Lotus House, East Japan, 2005**

top right: **Stone Plaza and Museum, Nasu-gun, Tochigi Prefecture, 2000**

bottom left: **Chokkura Plaza and Shelter, Takanezawa, Tochigi Prefecture, 2006**

bottom right: **Ginzan Onsen Fujiya, ryokan, Obanazawa, Yamagata Prefecture, 2006**

top left: **Z58 Zhongtai Box, facade,** Shanghai, China, 2006

middle left: **Adobe Museum for Wooden Buddha**, Shimonoseki, 2002

bottom left: **Asahi Broadcasting Corporation Headquarters**, rooftop sky garden, Osaka, 2008

top right: **Plastic House, Tokyo,** 2002

middle right: **Takayanagi Community Center,** Takayanagi, Niigata Prefecture 2000

bottom right: **Nagasaki Prefectural Art Museum**, Nagasaki, Nagasaki Prefecture, 2005

for nature and environmentally friendly architecture, Ando's buildings are dramatic in their use of light and have a strong presence and a powerful relationship to nature. Kuma's tend to be light and fragile, and appear to dissolve into their surroundings, making his erasing of architecture a poetic metaphor.[38]

By virtue of his unique and highly varied application of a broad range of materials, Kuma's architecture exhibits great variety. Indeed, just about every project by him appears different. Compare, for instance, the materials used in his Z58 Zhongtai Box building to those of the Masanari Murai Museum, the Plastic House, or the Takayanagi Community Center. The street facade of the Z58 is made up of horizontal bands of shiny metal planters with green ivy growing in them, placed in front of a glass wall. On the other hand, the Masanari Murai Museum features slim vertical strips of wood saved from the previous building on the site. The Plastic House, true to its name, is configured almost entirely of translucent glass-fiber-reinforced plastic, with equally translucent thermal-fiber insulation. The Takayanagi Community Center, like the pitched-roof vernacular architecture that surrounds it, is a wooden structure with a thatched roof, and locally produced waterproof kadobe-washi paper screens make up its exterior walls and even its floor. Recognizing the impressive variety in Kuma's work, the prominent Japanese historian Hiroyuki Suzuki has pointed out that he draws attention by being extremely prolific, in that each of his works has opened up a new horizon of expression. In this way, he exemplifies the highest creative potential of contemporary Japanese architecture.[39]

When possible, Kuma relies on local materials such as stone, wood, paper, and others available around or near the site where he is building. Sometimes his architecture appears to grow from the place itself. In turn, his materials contribute to the creation of those places by endowing them with special character and a particular intimacy, even when they are public in nature and large in scale. An example of this locally grown architecture is his Adobe Museum for Wooden Buddha in Yamaguchi Prefecture, where the soil dug out from the site was made into *hanchiku* (unfired bricks) and used in the construction. Then, in the Z58 building, he shrouded the facade in locally grown ivy; in doing so, he has envisioned a new kind of green architecture that is not only eco-friendly but also unusually attractive. This is even more so on the interior, where the multistory glass atrium behind the facade benefits from the presence of nature.

These solutions demonstrate Kuma's intention to produce ecologically sound buildings that both protect and enhance the environment. As part of such considerations, he frequently designs the rooftops of his large urban buildings as grass-covered surfaces or, wherever possible, landscaped and planted parks. In either case, these elevated landscapes provide good thermal insulation and thus save energy. His most extensive and impressive green roofscapes are atop the Food and Agriculture Museum in Tokyo, the Nagasaki Prefectural Art Museum, the Tobata C Block complex in Kitakyushu, the Asahi Broadcasting Corporation Headquarters in Osaka, and the Student Union Hall at Kyoto University of Art and Design.

Kuma is committed not only to preserving the environment, but increasingly, to preserving architecture as well. This may seem contradictory from a designer who started his career with the intention of erasing architecture, but sometimes saving a building (or part of it) is more beneficial to the environment than pulling it down and constructing another from scratch; it means

38. Kuma, "Digital Gardening," 6.

39. Hiroyuki Suzuki, "Position of Kengo Kuma," in Erickson, *Kengo Kuma: 2007–2008*, 24.

less labor, less energy, less costs, and less pollution. Several of Kuma's recent projects illustrate this strategy. The Z58 building is noted not merely for its green facade but also because its design is based on the reuse of a renovated structure, to which Kuma added new sections, including the entrance atrium. Recent examples of preservation include the Stone Plaza, the Nasu History Museum, the COCON Karasuma, and the Chokkura Plaza and Shelter.

The seamless blending of old and new is particularly striking in the Yien East/Archipelago, a private residence in Kyoto, where Kuma restored several traditional Edo-period structures, including a wooden gate, a Noh stage, and a small shoin-type residence; they were moved to the site from their previous location in Kanazawa, resulting in one of Kuma's most appealing domestic architectures. Or consider, for example, the small Masanari Murai Museum, built around the preserved core of the old residence of a noted Japanese painter. Here, Kuma used slim slices of worn-out clapboard siding from the original structure and arranged them vertically as a screen over the museum's exterior walls. Murai's old and rusting car, permanently preserved and parked within the shallow reflective pool in front of the building, contributes to an architecture of the surreal.

Indeed, materials play an increasingly prominent role in Kuma's architecture. In a discussion with Hiroyuki Suzuki, he said it this way:

> I do not know whether an architecture in which the form and silhouette disappear, leaving only materiality, is possible, but it is something I want to pursue. From the point of view of…conventional [logic], this is a contradiction. Until now in architecture, form and material have been connected, but I want to separate them.[40]

SENSORY DESIGN AND JAPANESE TRADITIONS

Kuma approaches each project first by thinking about materials.[41] He considers the location of the structure, the qualities of its place, and, of course, the function of the building. Although he seeks to neutralize the exteriority of a building, his designs are by no means intended to be neutral or indifferent. They acquire their particular character and often highly sensuous qualities not by means of strong iconographic forms or solid and permanent facades but through a perceptual field of intangibles, evoked by virtue of his special attention to materiality, tectonic precision, and spatial articulation as the architecture is exposed to the ever-changing conditions of light, views, sounds, tactility, and movement.

The broad range of these sensory qualities and the depth of meaning with which Kuma imbues his designs can be uncovered by the buildings' visitors only gradually. Appreciating the serenity and quiet beauty intrinsic to them requires patience and active engagement as they unfold slowly through the passing of time. In our age of instant gratification, Kuma's architecture invites us to slow down and take our time; only in this way can we discover the values and richness inherent in his designs. Pallasmaa was correct when he observed:

> [Kuma's] buildings give rise to an alert and sensuous feeling that enables us to become actively aware of the subtleties of the seasons, weather, light and human activities. Through repetitious patterns he creates hypnotizingly monotonous surfaces that highlight materiality, and evoke subtle and

40. Kuma and Suzuki, "A Return to Materials," in *Japan Architect* 38, 5.

41. Kengo Kuma, Q&A session after his lecture at the Art Institute of Chicago, October 9, 2008.

42. Pallasmaa, "Veils of Light," 22.

top left: **Masanari Murai Museum, the old car as sculpture in the garden, Tokyo, 2004**

top right: **Nasu History Museum, Nasu-Gun, Tochigi Prefecture, 2000**

left and below: **Yien East/Archipelago, West Japan, 2007**

changing sensations of transparency, reflection and levitation. Instead of making formal statements, he creates atmospheres that condition perceptions and feelings.[42]

Although his designs are obviously contemporary—one might even consider them modern in the best sense of the word—more so, his work is in close relation to traditional Japanese architecture. The value and relevance of tradition in the work of contemporary Japanese architects have been important issues in the architectural discourse in Japan since the country embarked on the road to Westernization and modernization in the mid-nineteenth century. Designers, critics, and theoreticians take divergent positions in the discussions, even today. While cultural heritage is difficult to exclude from the work of most Japanese architects, tradition does not always play an important role in their projects. In Kuma's case, he demonstrates great skill in integrating buildings into the environment and bringing them closer to nature, both of which are hallmarks of traditional Japanese architecture. Moreover, the sensuous quality of his designs is reminiscent of *sukiya*-style residences dating back to the early seventeenth century.

Sukiya architecture evolved from the rather disciplined and codified *shoin* style under the influence of the minimalist and informal *soan* (teahouse) architecture of the late sixteenth century, and it gradually began to dominate the homes of most social classes. Free from restrictive formalities, sukiya-style architecture expresses the individual taste and culture of the owner. While fostering a relaxed atmosphere and reflecting the sophistication of a "man of taste," sukiya-style interiors appealed to all of the senses. The attraction of sukiya architecture is attributable to its use of natural materials, such as its slender wooden structural frames, tatami floors, and sliding shoji and fusuma partitions made of paper, wood, or bamboo; it lacked excessive ornament and offered a sense of lightness. Above all, it fostered intimacy, particularly in its relationship to nature. Increasingly popular in the peaceful times of Edo period (1603–1868), the sukiya was, by and large, an architecture whose estheticism, by the latter part of the period, flourished in a "floating world" (*ukiyo*), and as such, removed from the realities of the political world.[43]

Kuma's architecture is at variance with this historic architecture insofar that within the Post-Bubble economy, his minimalist disposition and the rich experiential qualities of his architecture, along with its environmentally friendly attributes, are very much in keeping with the political arena of today. Indeed, Kuma successfully blends the best longstanding Japanese aesthetic sensibilities with those qualities of comfort required of contemporary life and provided by the latest technological advancements. His use of slats, for example, is reminiscent of *kooshi* (wooden latticework) and *sudare* (bamboo screens), common traditional devices that mediate between inside and outside while providing privacy. He designs most of these screens and other elements using high-tech materials, such as stainless steel mesh, and contemporary technologies, such as automatic and remote-controlled systems.

The emphasis on horizontal planes in many of his buildings, with the vertical boundaries disappearing in various ways, is also closely related to traditional modes of building. This is most visible in Forest/Floor, where the thin floor plane, like the ceiling that continues in large overhanging eaves, is prominently expressed, as the building is elevated above the ground in a forested area of Nagano Prefecture. Kenneth Frampton has said of it:

43. After centuries of infighting and fierce wars, Japan was unified by the Tokugawa Shogunate at the beginning of the seventeenth century. With the closing of the country to the outside world in 1639 until its reopening in 1853, the Japanese enjoyed an extended time of peace. During these times, however, the arts and architecture started to inbreed and eventually tended toward decadence. Sukiya-style architecture, like many other traditional forms of art, survived over the years and with various interpretations is rather common even today.

top: Interior of a traditional sukiya-style urban residence in Yanai, Yamaguchi Prefecture, Japan

middle left: Forest/Floor, Karuizawa, Nagano Prefecture, 2003

middle right: Ludwig Mies van der Rohe: Barcelona Pavilion, Barcelona, Spain, 1929

bottom: Lotus House, upper terrace, East Japan, 2005

This elegant diminutive house with a traditional shallow-pitched roof...
represents the convergence of a number of occidental and oriental mythic,
tectonic tropes at once, such as Le Corbusier's piloti, the Maison Domino,
etc; Mies Van der Rohe's Farnsworth House, but also, of course, the Japanese
timber...house tradition, which is here transposed into a house supported
by tubular steel columns and two cylindrical concrete piles, while the main
floor is visually screened by sliding...gratings.[44]

The house's disposition high above the ground gives it a surprising
affinity with Japan's most sacred Shinto shrine, the Ise-jingu.[45] Just like this
ancient architectural model, Kuma's house is designed with a veranda in front
and an outside stairway to the elevated structure; its size and proportions
are similar to that of the Shinto shrine; however, the house is built with a slender steel structure and large glass facades; it is transparent and open, as
opposed to the closed, boxlike log construction of Ise-jingu. Another out-
standing example of blending Japanese and modern architectural models is
Kuma's Lotus House. The serene beauty of the architecture, as in the case of
the revered Katsura Imperial Villa in Kyoto, is derivative of both its intimate
communion with nature and the elegant design of its constituent elements,
such as the reflective pool on the lower rooftop terrace and the shallow pond
with lotus flowers in front of the building. On the other hand, the layout and
articulation of details of the same terrace, the slim metal posts, and the
travertine patio reveal the modernist influence of Ludwig Mies van der Rohe's
1929 Barcelona Pavilion in Spain.

Kuma's penchant for redefining historic precedents holds true, even
in cases where the program or cultural context calls for something more
traditional. This was the case for his Noh Stage in the Forest, as well as for
several of his restaurants, like Waketokuyama in Tokyo and the Sake No
Hana in London. In these examples, Kuma challenged traditional models of
architecture, either by introducing a new spatial arrangement or innovative
construction technique, or through his material selections.

Such strategies are even more poignant in his growing number of small
tea pavilions. In each case, he was able to bring about a novel experience
for the traditional ceremony. The tearoom, with its tiny space and rustic minimalist design, has remained one of the most characteristic types of historic
Japanese architecture. During the turbulent times of Japan's Middle Ages,
in the fifteenth and sixteenth centuries, it served as the setting for the medi-
tative ritual of tea. Chado, the cult of tea, has survived and is practiced widely
today. It is cultivated in special "schools" according to various branches
of tea tradition.[46] But times have changed since tea drinking arrived from
China in the twelfth century, and this has resulted in an increase in the vari-
eties of settings. Today, many architects are eager to design new types of
tea pavilions.

Like many of his well-known mentors and peers, such as Isozaki,
Kurokawa, Hara, and Ando, Kuma has devised several teahouses, mainly as
exhibition installations for occasional tea ceremony demonstrations. They
all differ in concept, size, material, and construction. The Oribe Teahouse
is assembled from slices of corrugated plastic sheets, while the Modern
Teehaus in Frankfurt, sited within the compound of Richard Meier's Applied Art
Museum, is an inflatable structure of translucent fabric. The Casa Umbrella,
a pavilion in Milan, was constructed out of custom-made and zipped-together
large umbrellas of Tyvek fabric.[47] The most ingenious small design is the

44. Kenneth Frampton, commentary given
after Kuma's lecture at the Art Institute of
Chicago, October 9, 2008, transcript provided
by Frampton.

45. Representing the *shimmei-zukuri*-style
Shinto shrine architecture, the famous
Ise-jingu, established around the third century
AD, is Japan's most sacred shrine. It is
dedicated to Amaterasu-omikami, the sun
goddess, from whom the imperial family and
the entire nation were believed to be descended.
This architectural type is built high on piloti,
surrounded by an open veranda and covered
by a pitched roof. The innermost sanctuary
(*shoden*), along with the entire compound of
innumerable structures, is rebuilt every twenty
years as part of Shinto's renewal rituals. The
last such rebuilding in 1993 was the sixty-first.
In earlier history of the shrine, the intervals
between rebuilding were irregular, showing also
longer periods due to extended wars.

46. Among such "schools" are the *Ura Senke*,
Omote Senke, and *Mushanokoji Senke*. *Ura
Senke* is considered the commoner's tea, and
Omote Senke is the aristocrat's tea; these are the
two leading schools. *Japan, An Illustrated
Encyclopedia* (Tokyo: Kodansha International,
1993), 1535.

47. The Casa Umbrella is also informally called
Casa Kasa; the Spanish or Italian *casa* means
"house" or "home" and is phonetically similar to
kasa, meaning "umbrella" in Japanese.

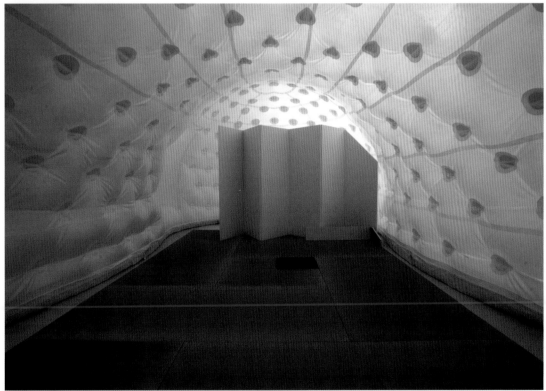

top left: **Waketokuyama, exterior facade detail, Minato-ku, Tokyo, 2004**

top right: **Oda Uraku: Jo-an Teahouse, Inuyama, Aichi Prefecture, Japan, 1618**

middle: **Modern Teehaus, Frankfurt, Germany, 2007**

left: **Sake No Hana, interior of the Japanese restaurant, London, United Kingdom, 2007**

Fuan Teahouse; Kuma floated a large helium-filled balloon in the air and suspended an extremely light and translucent super-organza veil from it to provide a celestial ambiance.

URBAN-SCALE PROJECTS AND PUBLIC SPACE

In the multitude of projects Kuma has worked on in recent years, a number of large urban complexes provide a sizable contrast to his many diminutive structures and installations; however, the differences between his small-scale works and urban-scale complexes are not limited merely to size. The vaster dimensions of a project would challenge any architect, requiring the transformation and transplantation of architectural ideas and design strategies, or the development of new ones to successfully execute such a large and complex task. An architect's mettle can also be measured by the skill and artistry with which he or she is able to resolve the difficulties inherent in the significant increase of scale and complexity of a project.

As mentioned earlier, Kuma began his career with the intention to erase architecture; however, a bigger building is considerably more difficult to erase. Large programs easily produce monumental volumes, posing difficulties for the designer. Kuma had to adjust his previously applied strategies and complement them with others. While keeping the overall forms of his buildings simple and minimal, he started to expand and redefine the idea of integrating inside and outside realms according to various given urban scales and conditions. In projects where the nature of the program or the tight site limited his options, he often returned to the application of vertical louvers, increasing their size and spacing according to the scale of the buildings. This is first seen in his seven-story Parking Structure in Takasaki, where two-foot-wide (sixty-centimeter) louvers of colored precast concrete and frosted glass are affixed to the steel frame at various angles. The result is a vibrant, breathing architecture that eschews the more ordinary and drab appearance of typical parking structures.

Kuma used a similar solution in his first truly urban-scale project in Tokyo, One Omotesando, the headquarters of several international fashion design companies. Due in part to the extensive program, the multistory building occupies the entire footprint of a highly irregular site in a dense urban area, and it features an extensive street facade composed of glass. To avoid complete transparency and to blend the building into the streetscape, he covered the glass surfaces with a system of closely spaced eighteen-inch (forty-five–centimeter) wood mullions. Situated along the famous zelkova tree-lined Omotesando Boulevard, the building benefits from the warm appearance of this wooden screen, and it offers a more intimate relationship with elements of nature in this urban environment, while providing a marked contrast to the glitzy fashion district around it.

In the huge Shinonome Apartment Building, also in Tokyo, the extensive use of vertical aluminum slats is similar to those of several of Kuma's earlier projects. Nevertheless, additional features begin to set his urban-scale projects apart from their smaller counterparts in significant ways. The building is part of a public housing development in which blocks were designed by different architects, including such renowned practitioners as Riken Yamamoto and Ito. Kuma's block is U-shaped and, as called for by the brief, it measures fifteen stories high. He took several approaches to mitigate the impact of this substantial volume. He called the first one a "communication atrium," which is, in effect, an open-air space, a gap inserted within the bottom part of the U-shaped site. Dividing the volume in this way, he arranged not only residential units but also small offices and home offices on both sides of the atrium, and he connected the two sides by numerous covered bridges. Additionally, he inserted multistory open and closed public spaces into the fabric of the building at diverse locations on all floors. Moreover, at the lower part of the complex, within the area left open by the U-shaped building, he designed numerous low-profile extensions, as well as small independent blocks, which feature public facilities serving both the residents and the public at large. The volumes of these common facilities connect with a one-story podium-like network, punctuated with internal courtyards and filled with shops, cafes, grocery stores, a health clinic, a kindergarten, and many others. The rooftop of this flat system of structures is designed as a green park. Kuma effectively modeled the interior and exterior spaces of this complex after the disposition of a small city, and in doing so integrated this large project into its surrounding urban enclave.

Kuma's method of breaking down a large program into its functional, spatial, or formal elements and then combining them into large but loose compositions seems to echo the work of his early mentor Maki, whose approach to urban projects involved achieving what he called "group form."[48] In this design strategy, Maki investigated the relationship between the parts and the whole, and he articulated it so as to create reciprocity between the two. In such organizations, individual elements generate a less predetermined whole by virtue of the flexible connections among them, which are provided through interstitial spaces. In turn, the whole, as an aggregate system or group form, ensures the viability of the parts. In the practical terms of designing large pieces of architecture or urban-scale projects, this means that outside spaces, usually public parks or plazas in-between architectural units, play a role as important as that of the units themselves. These spaces also have the capacity to form a matrix of intermediary zones between a large architectural complex and its environment, usually the urban realm.

Kuma began to receive commissions for larger urban-scale projects after the remarkable success of his previous works, the Ando Hiroshige Museum and the Stone Plaza and Museum, both completed in 2000, and following his winning the competition to design the Nagasaki Prefectural Art Museum in 2001. Regarding these two earlier buildings, it is important to point out that he was already implementing aspects of the methodology that he was to apply later in his larger projects. He designed the Ando Hiroshige Museum with a gatewaylike opening that provided not only the means of entrance to the building but also an open passage through it, connecting the small community in front to the small Shinto shrine behind. Almost the same intention is at work in his much larger museum complex in Nagasaki, one of Kuma's most successful designs in an urban setting. In this project, a small canal with flanking pedestrian promenades runs between two interconnected sections of the complex, bringing a part of the nearby sea, the port area, and the public realm of the city into the domain of the museum. The building opens up to this intimate, in-between urban space, both visually through large glass surfaces on the first floor and physically by means of additional entrances to the museum. These secondary entrances can be approached through shaded arcades, zones defined by the extension of the vertical stone louvers that populate the facades along the canal.

Two additional projects, the Ondo-cho Civic Center and the Asahi Broadcasting Corporation Headquarters, both completed in 2008, display

48. Fumihiko Maki, one of Kuma's university advisors in the late 1970s, authored several theses about various "collective forms" as the result of his investigating vernacular and traditional settlements in many parts of the world. In his *Investigations in Collective Form* (St. Louis: Washington University School of Architecture, 1964), he distinguishes between "compositional form," "mega form," and "group form," the first being the model of modern architecture, the second, structuralist and Metabolist, and the third, favored by him, vernacular or premodern architectures and settlements.

top left: **Nagasaki Prefectural Art Museum, Nagasaki, Nagasaki Prefecture, 2005**

top right: **Ando Hiroshige Museum, Bato-machi, Tochigi Prefecture, 2000**

middle: **Ondo-cho Civic Center, reflections of canopy in the glass, Kure, Hiroshima Prefecture, 2008**

left: **Asahi Broadcasting Corporation Headquarters, Fukushima-ku, Osaka, 2008**

several attributes that are comparable to those of the museum in Nagasaki and even the smaller-scaled Ando Hiroshige Museum. Like the Nagasaki Prefectural Art Museum, these complexes are located next to a body of water. The first is on the seashore near the city of Kure, while the other overlooks the Dojima River in downtown Osaka. Guided by these site conditions, Kuma shaped the complexes to mediate between nature in front and the city behind the buildings. He achieved this by filtering the two realms and their opposing qualities into his architecture through variably permeable boundaries. But due to the sheer size of these buildings, he also provided carefully calibrated large, tunnel-like openings through the bodies of these buildings to create more direct interfaces between divergent realms. Additionally, the Ondo-cho Civic Center features large lacy canopies, which serve as modified extensions of the pitched roofs. Acting as intermediary zones between the building, the outside public areas, and the seashore, these canopies reduce the scale of the building visually.

The Asahi Broadcasting Corporation Headquarters is slightly different. The building is composed of two crisply designed volumes, a tall one that matches the scale of the city behind it and a smaller one that faces the riverfront, together producing an L-shaped composition. Kuma rendered the facades of the smaller riverfront block as screens with a checkerboard pattern, similar to that of the Lotus House; however, the small panels are made of composite wood, rather than stone, which lends a vibrant warmth to the texture of the facades and creates a refreshing contrast with the tall white-panel-clad volume behind it. As he did with the Ando Hiroshige Museum, Kuma mediated between the city and the riverfront not merely on the level of spatial and visual reconciliation but also by way of the movement of people as they approach the river. From the street, a large wooden stairway leads through a gateway-like opening in the building to an elevated platform where visitors can take in excellent views of the river and the city beyond. From this platform, which is designed as a hilly, well-landscaped rooftop park, an additional wide stairway provides direct access to the riverfront. With such an impressive layout, Kuma choreographed an almost ceremonial public passage through the building's shifting sceneries. Moreover, the roof of the entire lower volume, a large private terrace, features another green park for the recreation of the company's employees. Echoing some of Kuma's early works, where he buried his architecture underground, here he has shaped these landscaped rooftops as topography.

The notion of architectural topography in Kuma's work has developed gradually and therefore appears in some of his earlier projects in nascent form. To single out but one example, the Nagasaki Prefectural Art Museum has a green grassy roof open to visitors, although the rooftop pool at his Water/Glass guesthouse in Atami can be interpreted as another form of topography. This is a feature that he repeated in his Baiso-in Temple in Tokyo and in the Z58 Zhongtai Box in Shanghai. Transforming the roofs of low-profile volumes within large urban complexes into public parks and plazas reaches its epitome in his recently completed Tobata C Block in the city of Kitakyushu. In this project, architecture as topography is not only extensive but also intricate, as these landscaped rooftops are replete with terraces, playgrounds, stairways, and bridges and are interconnected on various levels while extending into the interstitial spaces among the larger buildings.[49] To soften the contours of these tall structures, Kuma designed them as curvilinear plans and volumes. This project is impressive not only by virtue of its well-designed urban

49. The idea of architecture as topography is similar to that of the city as topography. Riken Yamamoto, another former student of Hara at the University of Tokyo, promoted the term in the 1980s. See R. Yamamoto, "City as Topography," *Japan Architect* (November/December 1986), 42. Kuma's interpretation of the idea is realized more as a green *topos* than merely as a public rooftop terrace or plaza.

architecture but also in that its open public places provide an ecologically sound solution.

Kuma's other project, the Stone Plaza and Museum, completed in 2000, is a small architectural assemblage that embodies perhaps the best early example of his articulating a design according to the principles of "group form." In this case, storehouses existing in a loose configuration on the site helped him considerably in creating a plan in which a matrix of courtyard plazas could be interwoven with architectural elements, while combining old structures with new ones. Considering the given locations of the existing buildings, he designed the museum's additions so as to shape the primarily open areas in between. These informal private spaces, defined partially by stone-paved surfaces with reflective pools, also connect to the larger urban realm, since the border between the museum compound and the street in front is marked only by a long stone bench along the water's edge. Discussing his intentions, he put it this way:

> The three existing buildings were of a matchless beauty; they had a delicate presence, but my attention was caught, above all, by the spaces between the structures…which were designed as focuses.[50]

Kuma's design methodology in the Stone Plaza and Museum can, in several respects, be regarded as a precursor to that of his most extensive project to date, a large-scale urban development in Beijing. Here too, he choreographed a fabric of interstitial spaces, among clusters of buildings, but on a much larger scale. The project occupies three city blocks in Sanlitun of the Chaoyang District, where numerous commercial, office, and residential complexes, most of them now completed, have been designed by several architects, each of whom was responsible for a group of buildings. In addition to designing most of the buildings, Kuma was in charge of producing the master plan of each block.

In this major project, Kuma introduced several new features in the areas of both urban design and architecture. Perhaps not surprisingly, these are as much the result of his response to the context of the Chinese city and its local culture, as they are extensions of his own investigations. One of his main concerns was to realize an urban environment with a human scale, despite the mammoth program. His first step toward this goal was to keep the height of individual buildings relatively low, limiting it within the taller and larger-scale layout of the Sanlitun SOHO block. As his second objective, he wanted to avoid plain and uniform facades, a typical feature of many urban complexes today. In Sanlitun Village North and South, he rendered the skin of simple architectural volumes as a system of panels in a mosaic-like pattern; like the skin of a chameleon, each panel changes color, translucency, and expression according to shifting light conditions or the position of the observer. At the Sanlitun SOHO development, building facades are wrapped in either vertically or horizontally arranged panels that appear like colorful bar codes. This treatment is directly related to those developed in earlier projects, such as the Parking Structure in Takasaki and the Suntory Museum in Tokyo.

Although the design of building envelopes is important in bringing about vibrant and rich urban realms, the most significant aspects of Kuma's latest projects in Beijing are his urban design strategies. His skillful arrangement of many architectural components and his choreography of movement

50. Kuma, quoted in Alini, *Kengo Kuma*, 102.

top left: **Tobata C Block, Kitakyushu, Fakuoka Prefecture, 2007**

top right: **Shinonome Apartment Building, Tokyo, 2004**

left: **Stone Plaza and Museum, Nasu-gun, Tochigi Prefecture, 2000**

bottom: **Sanlitun Village South, plaza, Beijing, China, 2007**

within large-scale public plazas are at the heart of his designs. In Sanlitun Village North, his inspiration was the typical traditional Chinese courtyard house. To reduce the extensive dimensions of the courtyard, defined by long blocks of buildings surrounding the site, he introduced four small volumes to create a sense of intimacy within the plazas. In the concentrically layered spatial arrangement, the innermost area is a sunken court planted with trees. The public realm also slips into interior spaces, as in the Opposite House Hotel, which is located at the south edge of the site; the multistory atrium is outfitted with urban amenities, including a fountain and a reflective pool. Furthermore, the restaurant and other facilities on the lower level are directly connected to another sunken court, accessible by a wide outdoor stairway. In designing the south block of Sanlitun Village South, his objective was to approximate the typically tight-woven, mazelike, and intimate street pattern of dense Chinese cities. It should be added that a similar street pattern characterizes Japanese cities as well, including the majority of Tokyo.

The Sanlitun SOHO project is more extensive compared to either Sanlitun Village North or South, as it features nine medium-height towers in addition to a series of low-profile wings, which include commercial, office, and residential units. Similar to the design of the Tobata C Block, Sanlitun SOHO's towers all have curvilinear plans and volumes, but each has a different shape and footprint. The irregular canyonlike passages among the buildings are also more generous in size, as they occasionally swell into larger public spaces featuring sunken plazas. The major attractions within these informal outdoor areas are the scores of trees and the constant presence of water, with shallow streams and fountains forming water-based playgrounds. The arrangement is reminiscent of the narrow streets and lanes in traditional rural and small urban settlements of mountainous Japan, where canals with streaming water run alongside pedestrian walkways.

IN LIEU OF A CONCLUSION

The purpose of my reviewing such a wide variety of Kuma's projects—ranging from his earliest to most recent, and from the smallest to the largest, with all of their various elements, strategies, and qualities—has been to investigate his architecture with regard to his stated intentions and theories and to shed light on the reasons behind his growing success. Emerging from this undertaking with increasing clarity, first of all, is perhaps an understanding that Kuma now regards "erasing architecture" more as a poetic metaphor and less as an actual possibility. While making the formal disposition of his buildings as nonintrusive as possible, he works toward achieving two intimately connected goals or conditions. On the one hand, he strives to establish close relationships between his architecture and its urban, natural, or cultural environment, whereby they merge as seamlessly as possible. On the other hand, he explores constructive and material conditions in order to nurture perceptual realms that are immaterial or phenomenological and, as such, appeal to all senses and impart profound experiences. Above all, however, his ultimate goal is to create meaningful human environments.

To achieve this, he appropriates the broadest possible architectural means. He does this without bias, freely but judiciously, with both the restraint and richness of an unpretentious creative artist. Accordingly, he has no concern or prejudice about stylistic norms or expectations.

I want to produce architecture freely without feeling constrained by specific techniques or methods.... More than, and prior to defining a style, what I desire is to create a certain type of place and a certain type of condition that can be experienced by the human body. Starting out from human sensations, I want to arrive at an architecture that utilizes everything, from traditional techniques to the most advanced technology.[51]

By all means, Kuma has already succeeded convincingly in arriving at such an architecture.

51. Kuma, quoted in Alini, *Kengo Kuma*, 102.

Ando Hiroshige Museum, interior, Bato-machi, Tochigi Prefecture, 2000

OLD AND NEW

REDEFINING TRADITIONS

Waketokuyama

Minato-ku, Tokyo
2003–4

above
**Exterior view, from the Gaien
Nishi-dori street**

opposite
Entrance and court

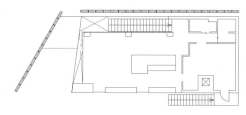

Second-floor plan

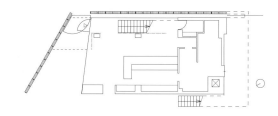

First-floor plan

Waketokuyama is a small, high-end Japanese restaurant in the Minami-Azabu area of Tokyo, near the Hiroo subway station. Because it faces the busy artery of Gaien Nishi-dori, whose heavy activity is out of step with the upscale atmosphere of such a restaurant, the building was designed to screen the patrons from the bustle and noise.

The facade is made possible by the use of extruded concrete. The material is cut to size, resulting in economical, lightweight prefabricated blocks called Asloc. As opposed to standard load-bearing applications, the blocks at Waketokuyama are horizontally mounted into a supporting flat-bar steel frame. The edges of this frame recede to give the blocks visual priority. This directly exposes the cross section of each, taking advantage of the material's construction process as an aesthetic texture. By keeping the "holes" of the block intact, the project reveals the part of the material that is ordinarily invisible. At night, light from the dining room glows through the porous surfaces.

One of these screen walls angles back into the site, leaving a gap between itself and the street-facing elevation. This configuration creates a small garden, an open-air anteroom, through which guests pass to enter the restaurant. Upon arrival in the dining area, visitors will have passed through a short succession of layers of material and space. The restaurant's 1,611 square feet (150 square meters) are split over two floors, accommodating approximately twelve people per floor.

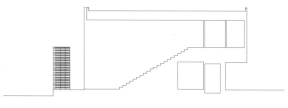

Longitudinal section

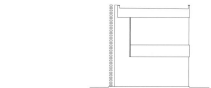

Cross section

Street-facing elevation

opposite, left
View through the glass entrance door

opposite, right
Detail of extruded-concrete facade

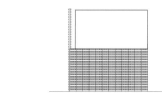

North elevation

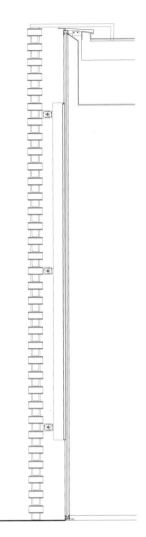

Section of extruded-concrete facade

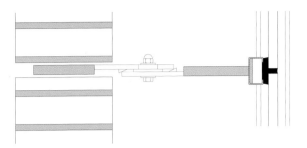

Detail of Asloc block screen

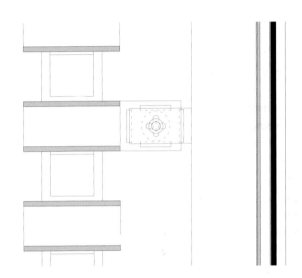

Detail of horizontal mounting

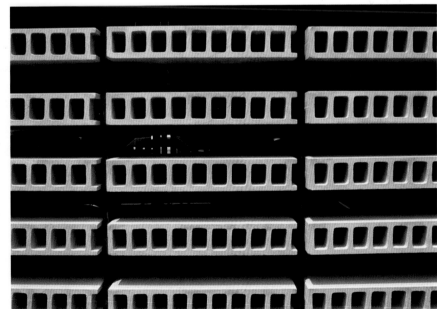

above
**First floor with a view of the
entrance court**

opposite
**Interior view of stairs and Asloc
block facade**

Cocon Karasuma

Shimogyo-ku, Kyoto
2003–4

above
**Exterior view, from Karasuma-
dóri street**

opposite
**Layered glass facade and street
entrance**

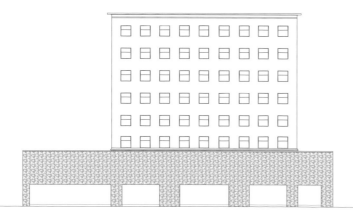

Elevation

Cocon Karasuma is the renovation of and small addition to the landmark Marubeni Building of 1938 in Kyoto's centrally located Shijo-Karasuma district. Once the head offices for a kimono company, the renovated building introduces an array of uses to bring new life to the previously neglected structure. It is now the location of assorted design and home goods shops, an independent cinema, offices, restaurants, and multi-use spaces, along with parking.

Because the building has particular historical significance, the project assumes the theme of "superimposed time." By overlapping new materials with old elements, Kuma created a system of strategic interventions that preserve the old building while enabling new uses. The most visible change is the new glass facade layered over the first two levels of the original building; the facade is illuminated to mark the presence of the building by night.

Film printed with an Edo-period cloud pattern, normally used for the paper covering of sliding doors, is sandwiched between two sheets of glass. The pattern was chosen from woodblocks preserved by the long-established karakami manufacturer Karacho. The combination of Edo-period graphics and modern construction techniques within an original 1938 building effectively unites various elements from different periods of time.

Inside, shops and several open galleries are arranged around the existing circulation core on the first two floors and basement. Restaurants and a large atrium occupy the annex of the original building, and a cinema and multi-use rooms are located on the third floor. The cloud motif continues inside the building as a graphic theme for many of the spaces.

left
Interior of entrance hall with glass-enclosed elevator lobby

right
View of the double-height atrium and cafe

Fourth-floor plan and up

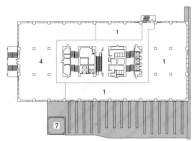

Third-floor plan

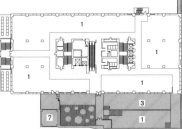

Second-floor plan

1 Shop
2 Event space
3 Atrium
4 Movie theater
5 EV hall
6 Office
7 Parking

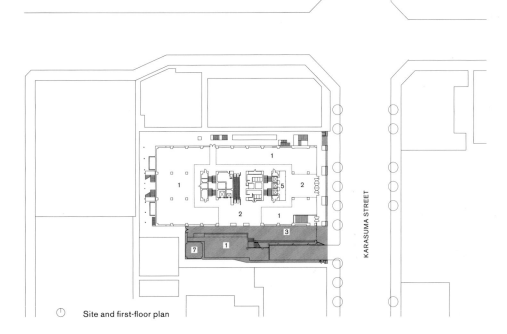

Site and first-floor plan

KARASUMA STREET

above
Exterior view from the street at night

opposite, top
The entrance at night

opposite, bottom
Interior of the entrance hall

Ginzan Onsen Fujiya

Obanazawa, Yamagata Prefecture
2004–6

above
Exterior view of embankment at night

opposite
The double-height entrance hall

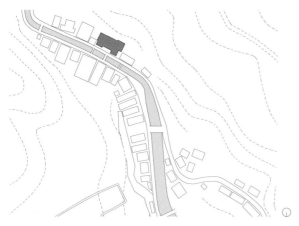

Site plan

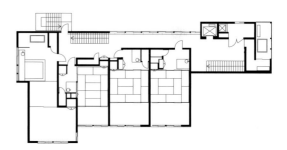

Third-floor plan

Second-floor plan

Tucked into an unassuming three-story structure, this guesthouse and thermal spa sits among a series of similarly scaled buildings in rural north Japan. The project's exterior updates the neighborhood's existing architecture, taking cues from whitewashed stucco and aged wood elements. This muted treatment presents the project in deference to the impressive locale: lushly vegetated mountains surround the site, and the primary stretch of buildings is organized along the embankment of a canal in meandering fashion.

The guesthouse's subtle exterior cloaks a comparatively varied interior, marked by layers and sequences. The approach leads one past a bridge, over the canal, and over a smaller footbridge and reflecting pool at the entrance. The entry is denoted by a succession of wood and glass screens. As a result, the lofty entrance hall can be reached without any easily discernible distinction between outside and inside. Sitting areas and a cafe flank this hall, and the spa's numerous bathing alcoves dot each of the floors. The upper two stories contain eight guest rooms. Each encompasses a main area sized at ten tatami mats, and each is sparingly outfitted with a long wooden tub, a counter, and a washbasin.

The understated protagonist in this project is a combination of light and texture. The spaces rely on diffuse and reflected light, tempered through one or more layers of screens. Approximately 1.2 million thin, knotted bamboo and vertical wood pieces compose these screens' filigree. The sources of light—even the artificial lighting—are hidden from view, creating a soft glow at the edges of the space, above or below, depending on the room. The relationships between screens, light, and views is reminiscent of Kuma's work at the Ando Hiroshige Museum, albeit at a smaller scale, with finer grain and texture in the screening.

First-floor plan

1   Water pond
2   Approach
3   Cafe
4   Entrance hall
5   Lounge
6   Office
7   Elevator
8   Kitchen
9   Staff area
10 Dressing room
11 Bath

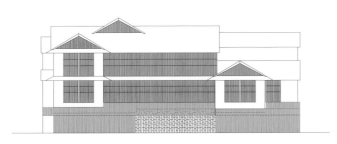

Elevation

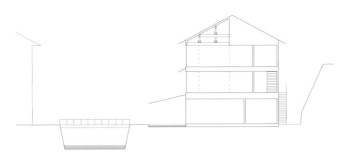

Section

top right
**View from across the small
Ginzan River**

bottom, left
Entrance hall

bottom, right
First-floor lounge

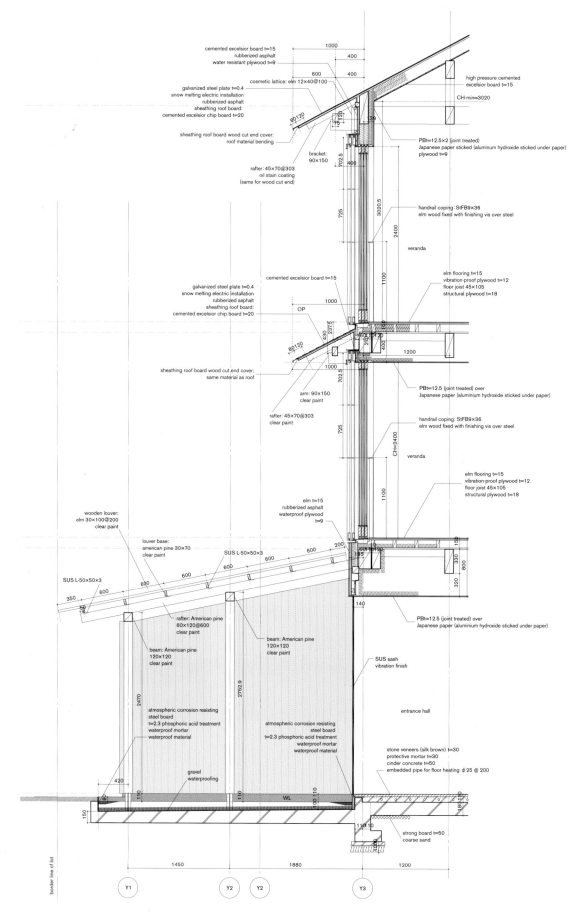

cemented excelsior board t=15
rubberized asphalt
water resistant plywood t=9

galvanized steel plate t=0.4
snow melting electric installation
rubberized asphalt
sheathing roof board:
cemented excelsior chip board t=20

sheathing roof board wood cut end cover:
roof material bending

bracket:
90×150

rafter: 45×70@303
oil stain coating
(same for wood cut end)

cosmetic lattice: elm 12×40@100

1000
400
600   400

80120

high pressure cemented
excelsior board t=15

CH-min=3020

PBt=12.5×2 (joint treated)
Japanese paper sticked (aluminum hydroxide sticked under paper)
plywood t=9

handrail coping: StFB9×36
elm wood fixed with finishing vis over steel

3020.5
2400
1100
725

veranda

elm flooring t=15
vibration-proof plywood t=12
floor joist 45×105
structural plywood t=18

galvanized steel plate t=0.4
snow melting electric installation
rubberized asphalt
sheathing roof board:
cemented excelsior chip board t=20

cemented excelsior board t=15

OP

1000

80120

sheathing roof board wood cut end cover:
same material as roof

arm: 90×150
clear paint

rafter: 45×70@303
clear paint

1200

PBt=12.5 (joint treated) over
Japanese paper (aluminium hydroxide sticked under paper)

handrail coping: StFB9×36
elm wood fixed with finishing vis over steel

CH=2400
2400
725
1100

veranda

elm flooring t=15
vibration-proof plywood t=12
floor joist 45×105
structural plywood t=18

elm t=15
rubberized asphalt
waterproof plywood t=9

wooden louver:
elm 30×100@200
clear paint

louver base:
american pine 30×70
clear paint

SUS L-50×50×3

SUS L-50×50×3

600
600
600
600
200

350
50

rafter: American pine
60×120@600
clear paint

beam: American pine
120×120
clear paint

beam: American pine
120×120
clear paint

150
330
320
800
140

PBt=12.5 (joint treated) over
Japanese paper (aluminium hydroxide sticked under paper)

SUS sash
vibration finish

entrance hall

2470

2752.9

atmospheric corrosion resisting
steel board
t=2.3 phosphoric acid treatment
waterproof mortar
waterproof material

atmospheric corrosion resisting
steel board
t=2.3 phosphoric acid treatment
waterproof mortar
waterproof material

stone veneers (silk brown) t=30
protective mortar t=30
cinder concrete t=50
embedded pipe for floor heating φ25 @200

gravel
waterproofing

420
60
150
110
110
100 110

WL

110 10

strong board t=50
coarse sand

border line of lot

1450
1880
1200

Y1   Y2   Y2   Y3

opposite, top
View at the entrance

opposite, bottom left
Detail of the stained glass wall

opposite, bottom right
Detail of the bamboo screen

Detailed section of the entrance hall

opposite
**Interior views of the first-floor
lounge**

top
**Second-floor guest room,
viewed through a glass wall**

bottom
Third-floor guest room

opposite
Special Japanese bath (*ofuro*)
on the first floor

above
Guest room interior

Sake No Hana

London, England
2006–7

above
**Interior of the first-floor guest
area**

opposite
**View of the forestlike wooden
ceiling structure**

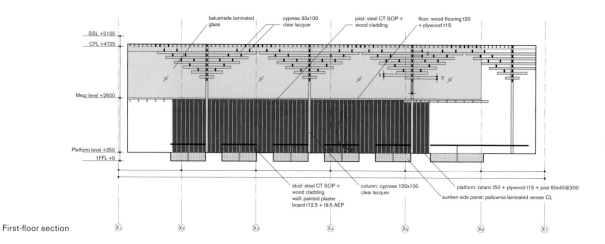

balustrade laminated glass
cypress 30x100 clear lacquer
joist: steel CT SOP + wood cladding
floor: wood flooring t20 + plywood t15

SSL +5155
CFL +4725

Mezz level +2600

Platform level +350
1FFL +0

stud: steel CT SOP + wood cladding
wall: painted plaster board t12.5 + t9.5 AEP

column: cypress 100x100 clear lacquer

platform: tatami t50 + plywood t15 + joist 60x45@300
sunken side panel: pailuwnia laminated veneer CL

First-floor section

London's Sake No Hana is a high-end Japanese restaurant. The project is an interior retrofit of the landmark Economist Building (1964), designed by Peter and Alison Smithson, in the St. James area of London. The intervention builds on Kuma's specific interpretation of urban planning: a three-dimensional method of arranging the city, distinct from the flat, plan-oriented zoning strategies of the 1960s. In this case, urban planning suggests the placement of objects and ways of layering new materials over old ones. Kuma describes the Smithsons' Economist project as a "mysterious landscape" of sprinkled stone, rather than merely stand-alone buildings. Sake No Hana expands upon this by distributing wooden pieces within the existing building, with delicate yet rigorous arrangements.

The restaurant organizes its dining and kitchen area over two main levels, and the core of the existing building acts as the structural and spatial anchor containing the central circulation. Guests enter a vestibule cloaked in darkly lacquered wood panels; from here, they choose either the sushi bar, wrapped to one side of the ground level, or continue via escalator to the main dining areas.

The second level of the restaurant exhibits a controlled palette of natural materials and invokes a distinctly Japanese means of constructing space within the modern English building. This is immediately obvious in the wooden interior finishes, doubling as the structure. Using bracketing as a primary method of connection—calling to mind Kuma's smaller Cidori installation in Milan, Italy—the project fuses the columns and ceiling into a single system. The wood framework rises above intimate banquettes and expands overhead into a gridded cloud. A mezzanine hovering just beneath this contains private dining spaces and a bar. At the perimeter, two layers of thinly cut bamboo screen the Japanese tatami seating areas with a moiré pattern of views and shadows.

from left
View of the streetscape;
the Economist Building;
night view of the restaurant;
entrance detail of wooden structure
illuminated at night

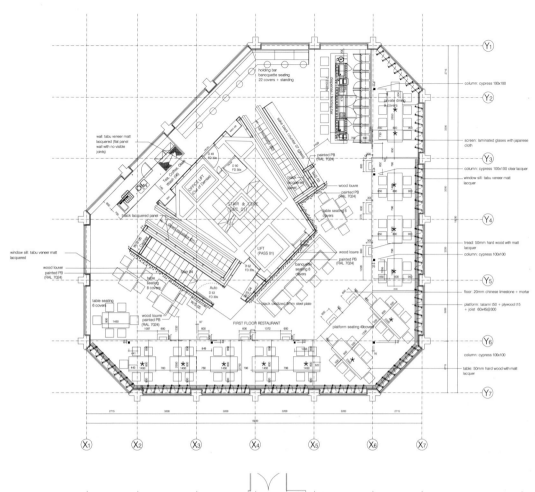

First-floor plan

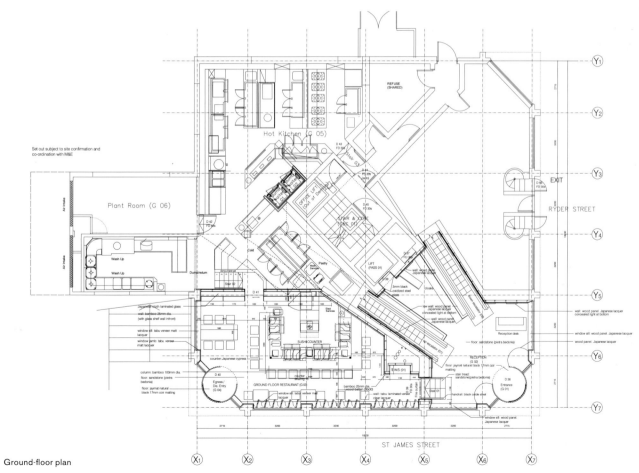

Ground-floor plan

opposite
**Detail of the double-layered bamboo
window screen, showing moiré effect**

above, left
**Interior of the ground floor in
evening light**

above, right
**Detail of wooden-board texture
of wall**

Yien East/Archipelago

West Japan
2005–7

above
View across the landscaped courtyard

opposite, top
**Seamless blending of inside and
outside at a corner of the building**

opposite, bottom
**The eastward view of the courtyard,
as seen from the building**

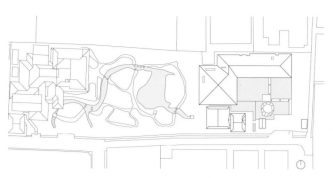

Site plan

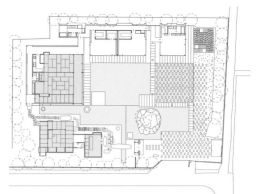

Ground-floor plan

This private residence is tucked away in a quiet neighborhood among old Buddist temples on the foothills of a traditional city in West Japan. The enclosed site is adjacent to a renowned garden by Meiji-period master gardener and landscape designer Jihei Ogawa (also known as Ueji).

The house is a collection of structures whose configuration casts importance on the exterior in-between spaces, placing them on the same level as the interiors. These structures roughly correspond to discrete daily functions, with water drawing everything together visually. Kuma calls this island of buildings an archipelago of architecture floating over the pond. A natural rock island with trees sits in the middle of the array, flanked by a grid of stones just above the water's surface. If water serves as the metaphoric connection, then a meandering path connects the various spaces, weaving indoors and out over the terrain, circumnavigating the water. This arrangement opens the house to its site.

The archipelago is of historical significance as well. The wooden gate and the shoin are careful reconstructions of elements from Taima-ji and Hannya-ji temples in Nara, respectively. Meanwhile, the noh stage was part of the Yokoyama House in Kanazawa before it was appropriated for its current location. These three Edo-period structures now embrace the functions of their new domestic context: house entry, tearoom, and living/dining. Three additional pavilion-islands corresponding to bathing, sleeping, and studying or contemplation create a semicircular formation around the water. They employ metal screens and glass beneath large eaves, the reflections of which echo the lightness of the older structures. Along with dark-burnt wood and rice-paper-sheathed walls, the newer counterparts firmly acknowledge older material and spatial traditions, without resorting to mimicry.

below, left
View of the garden, looking west

below, right
View over the pool, looking south

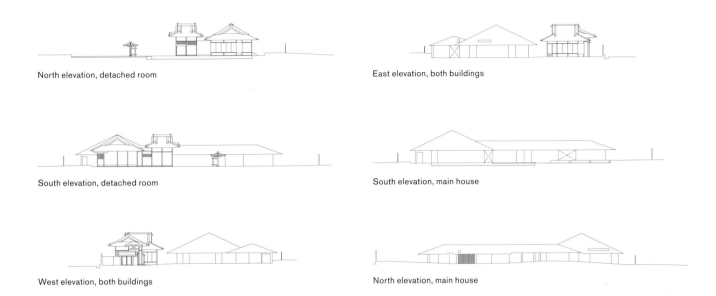

North elevation, detached room

East elevation, both buildings

South elevation, detached room

South elevation, main house

West elevation, both buildings

North elevation, main house

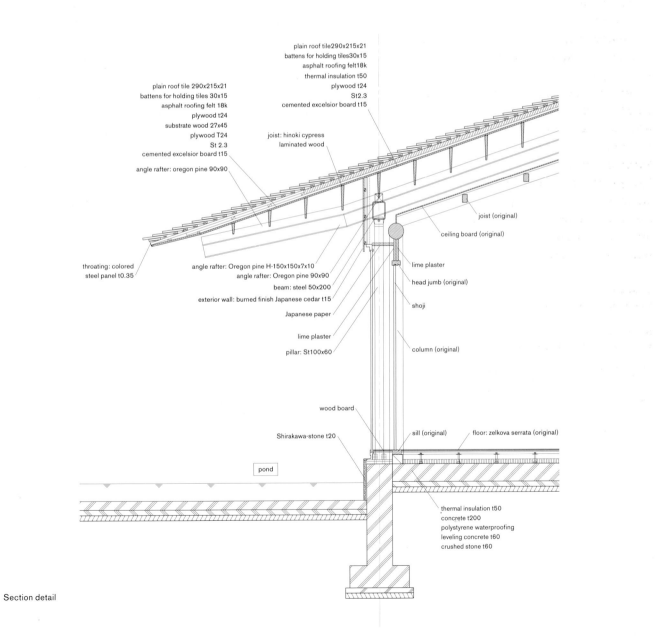

plain roof tile290x215x21
battens for holding tiles30x15
asphalt roofing felt18k
thermal insulation t50
plywood t24
St2.3
cemented excelsior board t15

plain roof tile 290x215x21
battens for holding tiles 30x15
asphalt roofing felt 18k
plywood t24
substrate wood 27x45
plywood T24
St 2.3
cemented excelsior board t15

angle rafter: oregon pine 90x90

joist: hinoki cypress
laminated wood

joist (original)

ceiling board (original)

throating: colored
steel panel t0.35

angle rafter: Oregon pine H-150x150x7x10
angle rafter: Oregon pine 90x90
beam: steel 50x200
exterior wall: burned finish Japanese cedar t15
Japanese paper
lime plaster
pillar: St100x60

lime plaster

head jumb (original)

shoji

column (original)

wood board

Shirakawa-stone t20

sill (original)

floor: zelkova serrata (original)

pond

thermal insulation t50
concrete t200
polystyrene waterproofing
leveling concrete t60
crushed stone t60

Section detail

above
**The garden seeps into the gap
between the buildings**

opposite, top
**Interior of the restored shóin building
to the south**

opposite, bottom
**View across the gap between two
restored traditional buildings**

opposite
**The "archipelago" of stepping stones
in the reflective pool**

top
Surface texture of the garden

bottom
**Patio between two parts of the
new wing**

Cha Cha Moon

London, United Kingdom
2008–9

above
**Entrance to the restaurant from
the mall**

opposite
**View of the long tables under
the bamboo ceiling**

Kuma was commissioned to design the Cha Cha Moon noodle bar. The restaurant is a new venture by restaurateur Alan Yau, who is also responsible for the similarly casual Wagamama noodle restaurant concept. In the same spirit, this effort offers affordable, everyday Chinese fare in a simple but refined atmosphere. The project is located at the top level of London's Whiteleys Shopping Centre destination, among other cafes and catering amenities. A single dining space accommodates approximately 140 people and is visible from the shopping concourse through a facade of glass, brightly colored polycarbonate panels, and mirrors. Custom-fabricated linear bamboo tables and dark metal benches seat small groups in communal fashion. The kitchen and serving counter flank one side of the central space, while a bar occupies the other side. An expansive bamboo ceiling dominates the project, drawing visitors into the dining area while undulating over tables and then swooping downward to form the back wall of the space. Suspended 2.3-inch (six-centimeter) bamboo rods are spaced at 4.7 inches (twelve centimeters) to highlight the dynamism and lightness of the ceiling's wavelike form. Thus, the bamboo ceiling unifies the restaurant's space and reinforces the shared dining experience. As added emphasis, mirrored panels visually increase the size of the main room, with the overhead bamboo seeming to extend limitlessly to either side.

top
Atrium of the mall, with the restaurant on the second floor

bottom
Double-layered glass partition with inner layer of aluminum honeycomb

opposite
Detail of the bamboo screen on the wall and ceiling

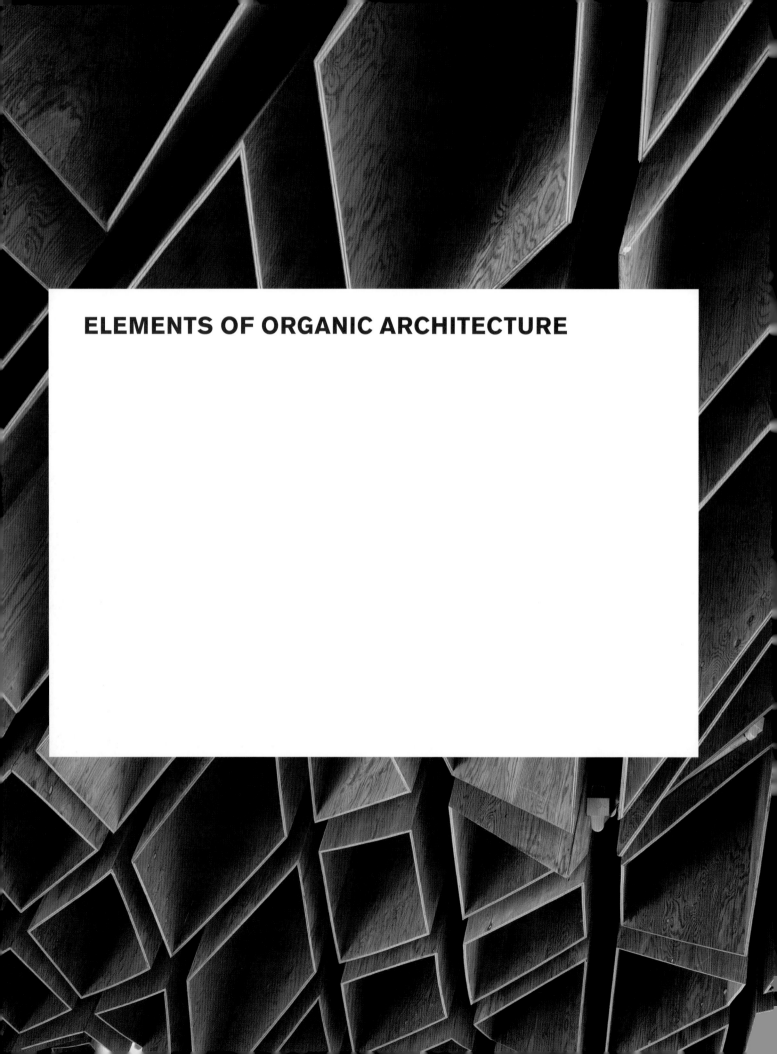

ELEMENTS OF ORGANIC ARCHITECTURE

BUILDING IN WOOD

Yusuhara Town Hall

—

Yusuhara, Kochi Prefecture
2004–6

above
Exterior view from southwest

opposite
**Interior view of the wooden structure
in the entrance hall**

This project is situated on Shikoku, the smallest of Japan's four primary islands. As the town hall for the township of Yusuhara, it includes space for hosting traditional Japanese performances and festivals, as well as other civic activities. The project utilizes locally harvested sugi, or Japanese cedar, as the primary building material. Beams, columns, and other wooden members spaced at the maximum structural dimensions allowable by building code make this one of Japan's largest wooden town halls. Double lattices of engineered, laminated lumber span fifty-nine feet (eighteen meters), creating a large atrium for the town's activities. Cedar panels in combination with aluminum and low-e composite glazing are configured into a horizontal grid on the facade.

Large operable doors on the front facade open in a fashion similar to an airplane hangar, connecting the large interior to the outdoor plaza, extending the hall's main space into the town. The atrium also serves as an interior plaza, providing shelter during the region's harsher seasons. The hall's other spaces—a bank, offices for several township departments, and meeting rooms—are organized around the atrium on two floors.

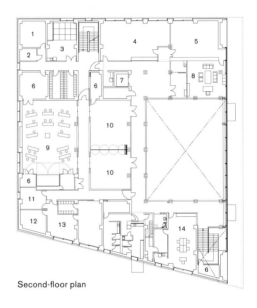

Second-floor plan

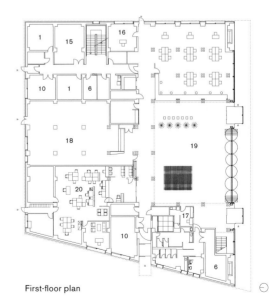

First-floor plan

1	Archive	11	Assembly president's room
2	EPS	12	Assembly archive
3	Restroom	13	Assembly secretary's room
4	Environmental improvement, industry promotion department	14	Chamber of commerce and industry office
5	Disaster prevention council office	15	Computer room
6	Storage	16	Office
7	EV	17	Night duty room
8	Major office	18	Tenant (bank)
9	Conference room	19	Atrium
10	Meeting room	20	JA

top, from left
**Remote view of the building;
external and internal views of
the open entrance hall**

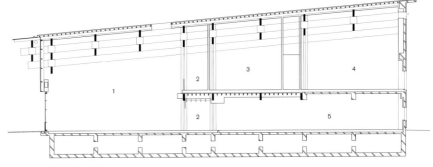

1 Atrium
2 Corridor
3 Meeting room
4 Conference room
5 Bank

Section

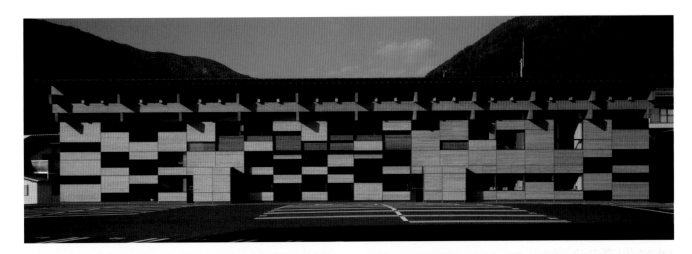

top
South facade

bottom, left
Interior view of perforated facade

bottom, right
**Small performance stage in the
entrance hall**

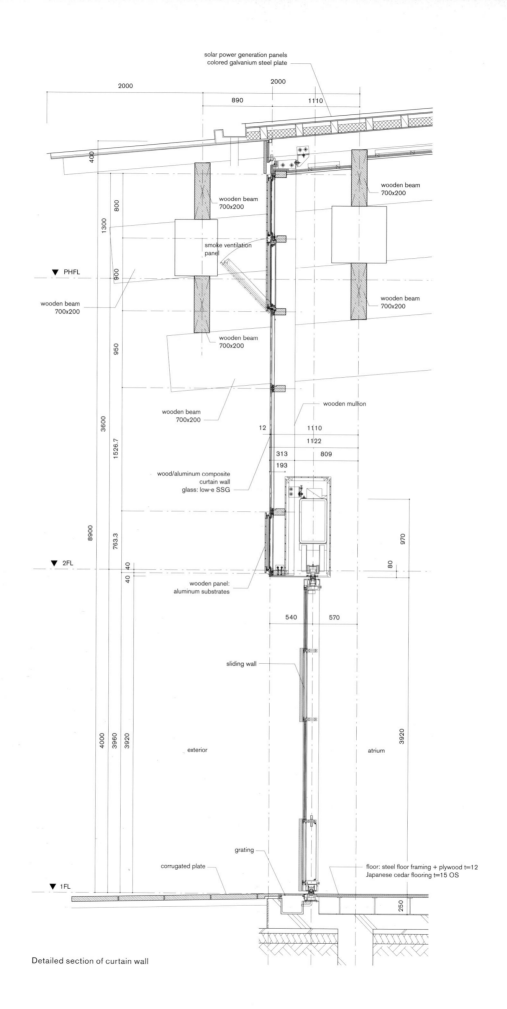

solar power generation panels
colored galvanium steel plate

2000

2000

890

1110

400

800

1300

wooden beam
700x200

wooden beam
700x200

900

▼ PHFL

smoke ventilation
panel

wooden beam
700x200

wooden beam
700x200

950

wooden beam
700x200

wooden mullion

3600

1526.7

wood/aluminum composite
curtain wall
glass: low-e SSG

12

1110

1122

313

809

193

8900

970

763.3

80

▼ 2FL

40

40

wooden panel:
aluminum substrates

540

570

sliding wall

4000

3960

3920

exterior

atrium

3920

grating

floor: steel floor framing + plywood t=12
Japanese cedar flooring t=15 OS

corrugated plate

▼ 1FL

250

opposite
**Detail of pattern on
south facade, with
entrance closed**

Detailed section of curtain wall

Y-Hutte

Karuizawa, Nagano Prefecture
2005–6

above
Exterior view from southwest

opposite
Interior view with wood-burning stove

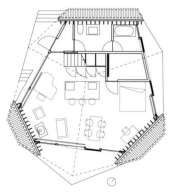

First-floor plan

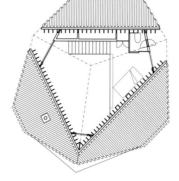

Second-floor plan

The Y-Hutte is a small villa, near Karuizawa, that occupies a modest 790.1 square feet (73.4 square meters) of a vast, heavily wooded site. The villa is defined by its triangular faceted roof and organized as a single space with living, dining, cooking, and sleeping areas on the ground floor, along with a study and a music area. A loft contains the sleeping area for guests, and tucked beneath the edges of the roof are additional supporting spaces.

Kuma designed the villa as a reinterpretation of Marc-Antoine Laugier's "primitive hut." In fact, the Y-Hutte reduces the archetypal shelter even further—here, shelter dispenses with columns, as well, leaving the roof as the primary element.

With architectural devices pared down to a minimum, wood becomes the governing material and metaphoric theme of the villa. The texture of the exterior is composed of numerous pieces of Oregon pine, spaced at increments to allow for airflow and visual lightness. Inside, this material forms a series of rafters and joists reaching upward, reproducing the feeling of being surrounded by a dense forest. Scandinavian pine floors complement the palette.

The Y-Hutte depends solely on triangles as its basic geometric unit. This theme is carried consistently from the polyhedral roof to the outline of the foundation. The villa's volume is itself a tetrahedron with its vertices truncated to create the entry and to open the house to surrounding views.

South elevation

West elevation

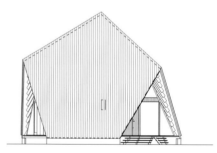

North elevation

East elevation

above
Detail of roof and terrace

right
**Interior views, with kitchen counter
and bathroom sink**

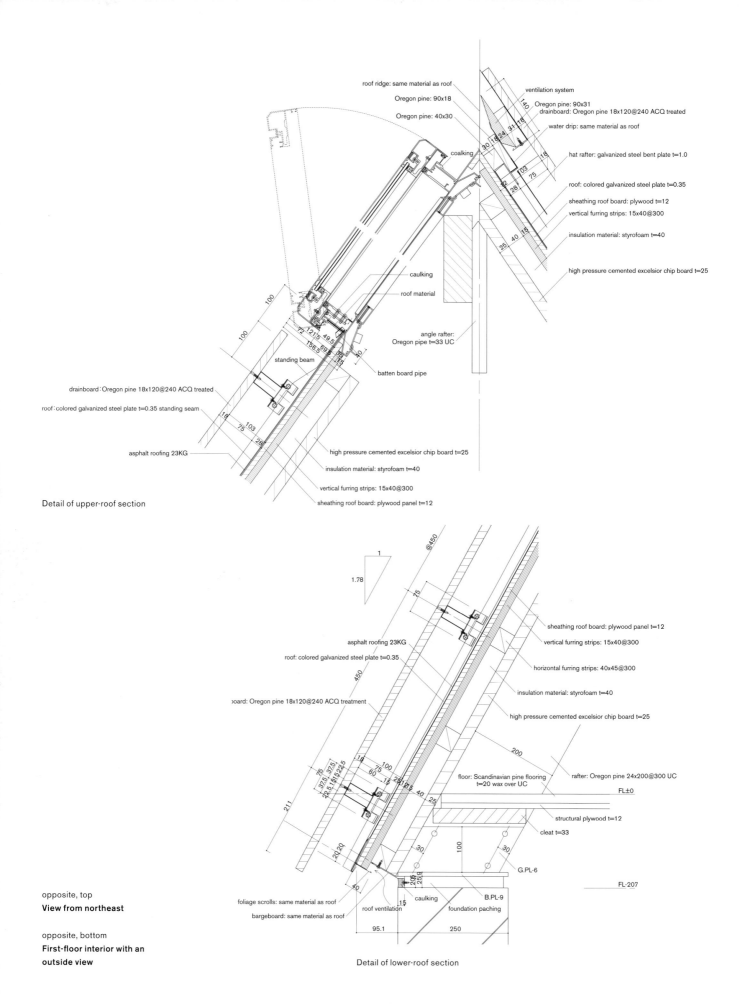

roof ridge: same material as roof

Oregon pine: 90x18

Oregon pine: 40x30

coalking

ventilation system

Oregon pine: 90x31

drainboard: Oregon pine 18x120@240 ACQ treated

water drip: same material as roof

hat rafter: galvanized steel bent plate t=1.0

roof: colored galvanized steel plate t=0.35

sheathing roof board: plywood t=12

vertical furring strips: 15x40@300

insulation material: styrofoam t=40

high pressure cemented excelsior chip board t=25

caulking

roof material

angle rafter:
Oregon pipe t=33 UC

batten board pipe

standing beam

drainboard: Oregon pine 18x120@240 ACQ treated

roof: colored galvanized steel plate t=0.35 standing seam

asphalt roofing 23KG

high pressure cemented excelsior chip board t=25

insulation material: styrofoam t=40

vertical furring strips: 15x40@300

sheathing roof board: plywood panel t=12

Detail of upper-roof section

asphalt roofing 23KG

roof: colored galvanized steel plate t=0.35

board: Oregon pine 18x120@240 ACQ treatment

sheathing roof board: plywood panel t=12

vertical furring strips: 15x40@300

horizontal furring strips: 40x45@300

insulation material: styrofoam t=40

high pressure cemented excelsior chip board t=25

rafter: Oregon pine 24x200@300 UC

floor: Scandinavian pine flooring
t=20 wax over UC

FL±0

structural plywood t=12

cleat t=33

G.PL-6

FL-207

foliage scrolls: same material as roof

roof ventilation

caulking

B.PL-9

foundation paching

bargeboard: same material as roof

opposite, top
View from northeast

opposite, bottom
**First-floor interior with an
outside view**

Detail of lower-roof section

Hoshinosato Annex

Kudamatsu, Yamaguchi Prefecture
2004–6

above
Exterior view from southeast

opposite
Detail of east facade in the evening

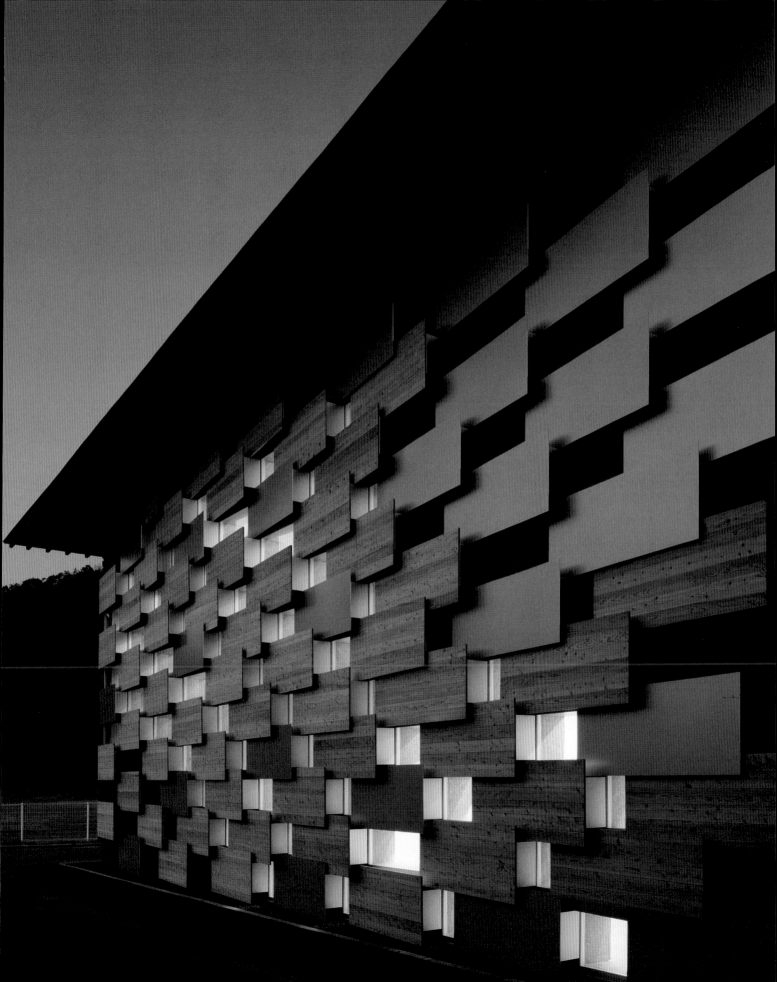

An addition to a nursing home, Hoshinosato Annex augments the original structure by providing a new set of rooms and common areas. Building and fire safety codes, along with design considerations for the elderly, were interpreted as opportunities for creating inventive facades and casual interiors.

Although compositional in pattern, the facade displays an underlying logic. It was necessary, due to building code, to place aluminum panels alongside wooden ones on the east wall. Rather than assigning clear zones for each material, the panels were dispersed with gradations of aluminum, and they were lapped at angles, with openings for the windows. The south facade, unburdened by these requirements, was assembled in a different manner. Here, loosely arranged wood planks bring the wall and rain shutters together into a unified system. The result is an airy, striated wall that casts shifting patterns of shadow throughout the day.

The annex's common areas are located on two floors and include a kitchen/pantry area, bath, and salon lounge. Ten bedrooms on each floor are organized on either side of the building's spine. Instead of acting as a wide corridor, as with many other buildings of this type, the space is large enough to provide the facility with a living area on each floor. Also, to infuse the building with warmth, low-cost wooden oriented-strand-board panels were applied to the interior surfaces of these common areas.

above, from left
Interior of room; common area between rooms

opposite, top left
View of south facade

opposite, top right
Daytime interior view with stairway

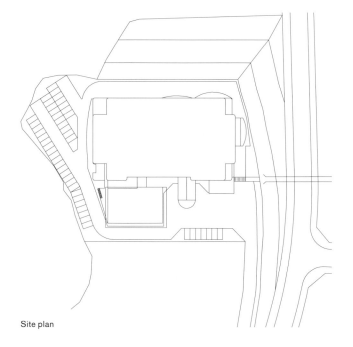

Site plan

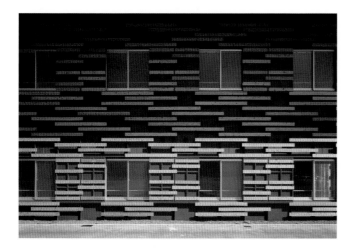

Second-floor plan

1 First-floor connection
2 Common living
3 Pantry
4 Saloon
5 Bedroom
6 Restroom
7 Bathroom
8 Terrace
9 Second-floor bridge

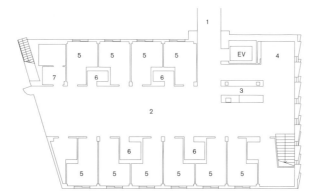

First-floor plan

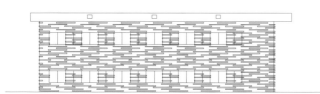

South elevation

East elevation

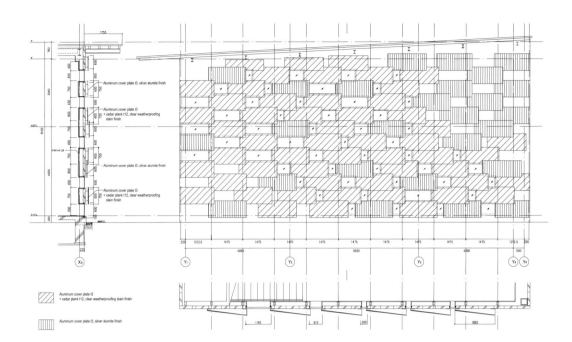

East elevation

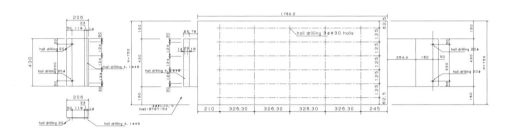

Aluminum cover plate
(unfold)

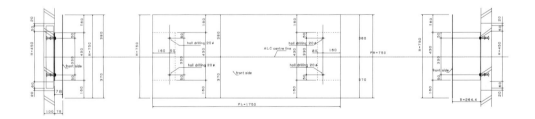

Aluminum cover plate
(elevation)

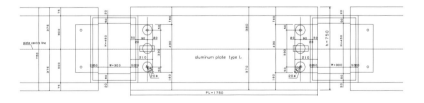

Aluminum cover plate
(details)

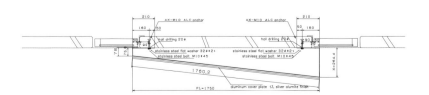

opposite
Detail of east facade

Ondo-cho Civic Center

Kure, Hiroshima Prefecture
2004–8

above
Second-floor terrace under the canopy of the extended roof

opposite, top
Exterior view of eaves and wide stairway

opposite, bottom
Detail of facade

Occasionally when approaching a large project, Kuma first focuses on a small detail. By incorporating a roof tile common to the city of Kure, the Ondo-cho Civic Center exemplifies this approach. Looking northeastward over a bay of the Inland Sea, the site is surrounded by numerous traditional roofs. Canals border the site to the north and split the project into two uneven volumes; while a breezeway opens between these halves, offering a glimpse of the bay in the distance.

The vast roof system unifies the building and gathers several community spaces beneath it. Authentic Japanese tiles are spaced at intervals to provide expanses of modulated views. By employing both semicircular and rectangular tiles, the result appears both natural and highly ordered. Arranged as a slanting louver system, parts of the roof extend all the way to the ground, providing shade and privacy to the spaces behind it. Also, the appearance of individual units of material—what Kuma calls visible "particles"—reduces the perceived sizes of these volumes.

The roof tiles form one kind of louver for the exterior, but another type infuses the interiors with a consistent texture. Thin baffles of wood in varying dimensions cover the interior walls of the major spaces, dovetailing with similar pieces on the ceiling and draping downward along the edges of the rooms. The ground level of the larger volume contains the entrance lobby, the foyer for a small library, and the branch office of Kure's city hall. The second level has a spacious auditorium and stage for community events. The smaller volume contains multipurpose rooms on the upper level and parking at ground level.

above
Remote views across the bay

Site plan

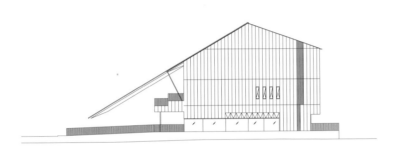

West elevation

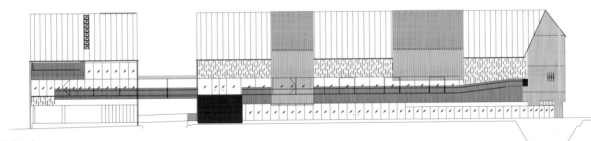

North elevation

top, left
View of breezeway over the canal

top, right
Interior stairway

opposite
Views of baffled wood detailing

above
Second-floor multipurpose hall

JR Hoshakuji Station
—

Takanezawa, Tochigi Prefecture
2005–8

above
View of station from the west

opposite
Looking up at covered stairway

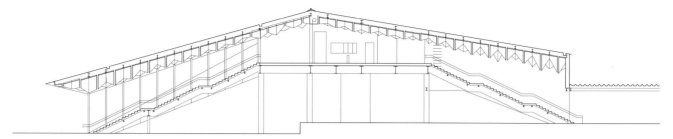

Section

A renovation of the existing train station located next to the Chokkura Shelter and Plaza in Takanezawa, the two-platform structure is part of the JR Tohoku train line connecting the township to the regional railway branches. In addition to the platforms and entrance hall, it includes the stationmaster's office and basic facilities such as restrooms, waiting areas, and elevators.

The project revises the former structure such that the final result is a connective gateway or aperture, rather than a static box. The eastern side of the station—facing Chokkura Plaza—connects the east and west sides of Takanezawa, which were once divided by the barrier-like railway. Thus, the primary body of the station levitates perpendicular to and above the tracks.

Following the flow of people from the station's entrances to the platforms is a continuous ceiling "fabric" made of Lauan plywood and arranged within a steel diamond-shaped grid, similar to the facade motif of the Chokkura Shelter and Plaza. Inside the station, substituting wood for stone creates a softer character, and the diamond shapes provide graphic continuity with the adjacent plaza. With indirect lighting passing between the gaps in the ceiling, its surface appears alternately warm and rough, angular and fluid.

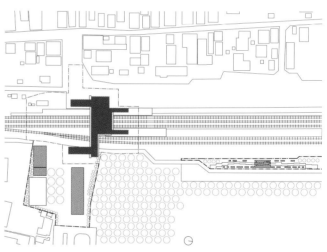

Site plan

opposite, top left
View from the south

opposite, top right
The station and adjacent Chokkura Shelter and Plaza

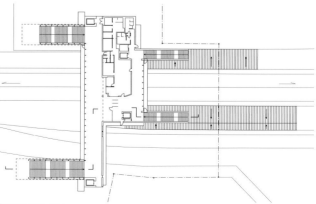

Second-floor plan

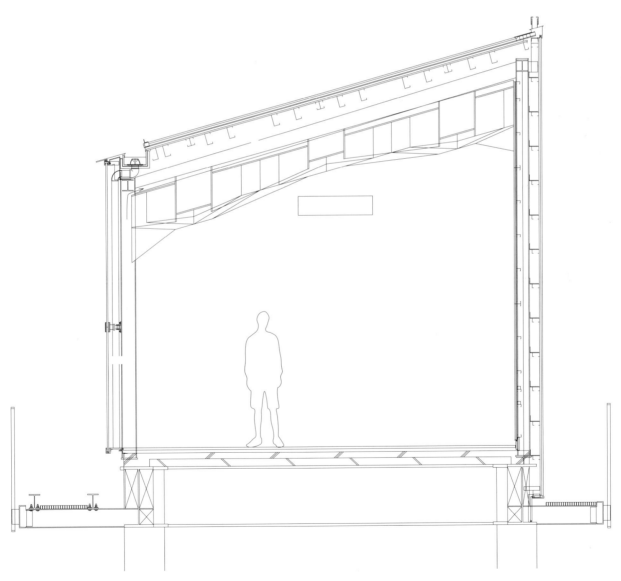

Section of overpass

top
**Covered stairway on the south side
of the station**

bottom
Second-floor pedestrian overpass

opposite
**View of diamond-shaped grid
pattern of ceiling**

CHALLENGING MATERIAL

SPATIAL FILTERS IN STONE

Food and Agriculture Museum

Setagaya-ku, Tokyo
2002–4

above
Exterior view

opposite, top
**View of first-floor interior
with staircase**

opposite, bottom
**Interior view of glass curtain
wall and stone louvers**

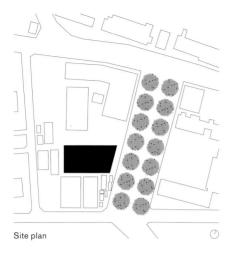
Site plan

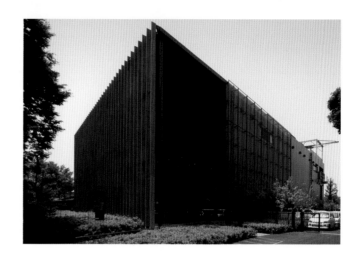

Located on the campus of Tokyo University of Agriculture, in the Setagaya ward, this research facility contains laboratories and offices in addition to galleries and exhibition rooms. The main areas are distributed across three floors, and a roof garden functions as an open-air agricultural laboratory.

In a gesture that opens the building visually to the exterior, the entrance hallway runs behind a facade of vertical stone louvers. A mezzanine with additional exhibition areas floats above, and the third floor houses laboratories and research areas. Since the facility enables research into natural processes, Kuma sought to connect architecture with nature. He achieved this by using materials that are softened by the environmental processes that affect plants. The series of stone louvers along street-level is designed as an abstraction of the parallel row of zelkova trees along the facade. Made of Ashino stone, a soft, highly absorbent material, the louvers register the effects of weather over time. Stone in 1.38-inch (3.5-centimeter) slabs work in tandem with 1.42-inch (3.6-centimeter) solid-steel plates, and the slats are set at angles that provide optimum shade to the south and east facades. In addition to these stone louvers, the building exposes its details, where possible, in order to exhibit the logic of its construction and the nature of the project. In these ways, Kuma explains, the project synchronizes architecture and nature.

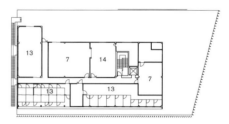
Fourth-floor plan

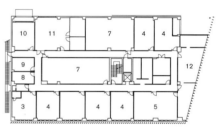
Third-floor plan

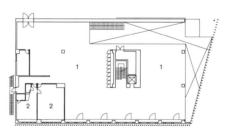
Second-floor plan

top, right
View from northeast

opposite
Entrance hall and lobby
viewed from above

1	Exhibition space	8	Night-duty room
2	Conference room	9	Incubation room
3	Seminar room	10	Specimen room
4	Research room	11	Laboratory
5	Reference room	12	Office
6	Waste room	13	Breeding room
7	Storage room	14	Electrical room

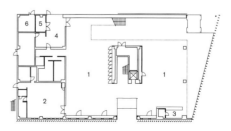
First-floor plan

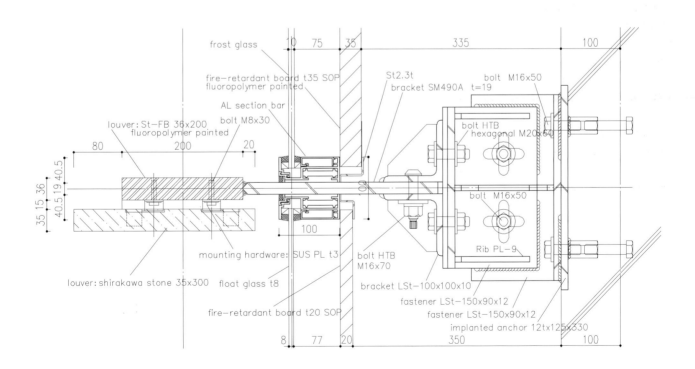

frost glass

fire—retardant board t35 SOP
fluoropolymer painted

AL section bar

louver: St—FB 36x200
fluoropolymer painted

bolt M8x30

St2.3t

bracket SM490A t=19

bolt M16x50

bolt HTB
hexagonal M20x60

bolt M16x50

Rib PL−9

10 75 35 335 100

80 200 20

35 15 36

40.5 19 40.5

100

mounting hardware: SUS PL t3

bolt HTB
M16x70

louver: shirakawa stone 35x300

float glass t8

fire−retardant board t20 SOP

bracket LSt−100x100x10
fastener LSt−150x90x12
fastener LSt−150x90x12
implanted anchor 12tx125x330

8 77 20 350 100

Aluminum and steel curtain-wall side detail (east side)

Lotus House

East Japan
2003–5

above
**External view of house and lotus pond
from the west**

opposite
**Screen of thin-travertine panels in a
checkerboard pattern**

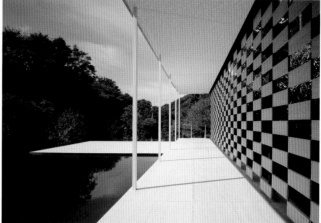

The Lotus House is a private vacation residence in a remote southern city of East Japan. Mountains and woods surround the house, and a small river borders one edge of the site. The house sits adjacent to but above the level of the river, so that only the sound of the stream drifts upward and into the project's spaces. Water rises to the edge of the house in the form of a long, thin reflecting pool containing numerous lotus plants.

A diaphanous skin of 1.2-inch (three-centimeter) travertine panels cloaks the exterior of the project. These panels, measuring 7.9 by 23.6 inches (twenty by sixty centimeters), converge in a checkerboard grid, alternating with voids. The pattern is held in place by thin stainless-steel elements spliced precisely between the travertine so that they recede visually and the stone appears suspended in air. Furthermore, the entire screen assembly hangs from the primary structure and sways lightly with the wind. In this way, the project transforms a seemingly heavy material into architectural filigree.

At the heart of this project lies a large, open-air room that divides the program into two wings. One contains all of the living spaces, the kitchen, bathrooms, sleeping quarters, and garage; the other houses a double-height studio with a library, piano, and sitting area. The central outdoor room opens out onto the adjoining pool, allowing air to pass through the volume of the building, reconnecting the living spaces with the surrounding landscape— a living room open to the elements.

top, left
View from the garden entrance

top, right
Rooftop deck and pool on the second floor

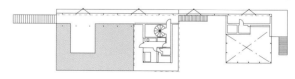

Second-floor plan

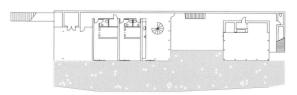

First-floor plan

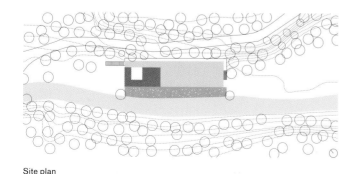

Site plan

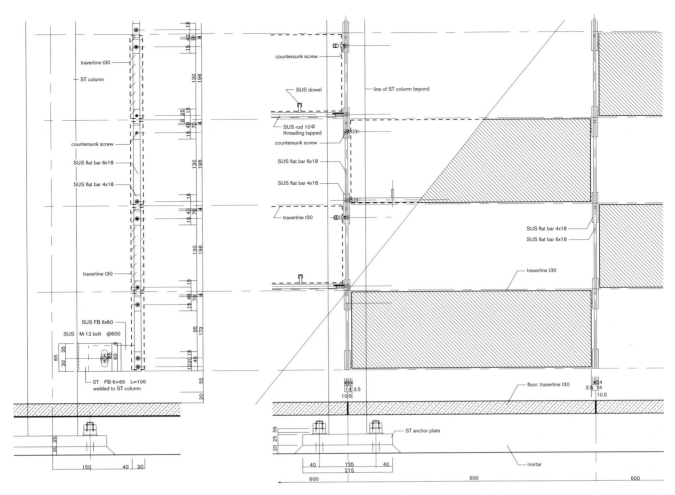

travertine t30
ST column
countersunk screw
SUS flat bar 6x18
SUS flat bar 4x18
travertine t30
SUS FB 6x60
SUS M-12 bolt @600
ST FB-6×65 L=105 welded to ST column

countersunk screw
SUS dowel
SUS rod 10Φ threading tapped
countersunk screw
SUS flat bar 6x18
SUS flat bar 4x18
travertine t30
line of ST column beyond

SUS flat bar 4x18
SUS flat bar 6x18
travertine t30
floor: travertine t30
ST anchor plate
mortar

Detail of travertine screen

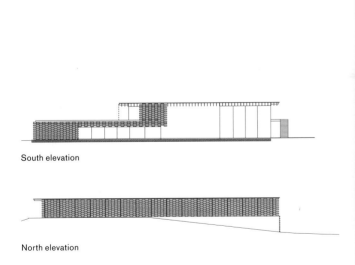

South elevation

North elevation

right
**Screen as mediator between
inside and outside**

opposite
View from the south

above
**Open-air room between two parts
of the house**

above
Interior of the open-air patio

opposite, top
Large living room with outside views

opposite, bottom
**View of the lotus pond from the
open-air patio**

Chokkura Plaza and Shelter

Takanezawa, Tochigi Prefecture
2004–6

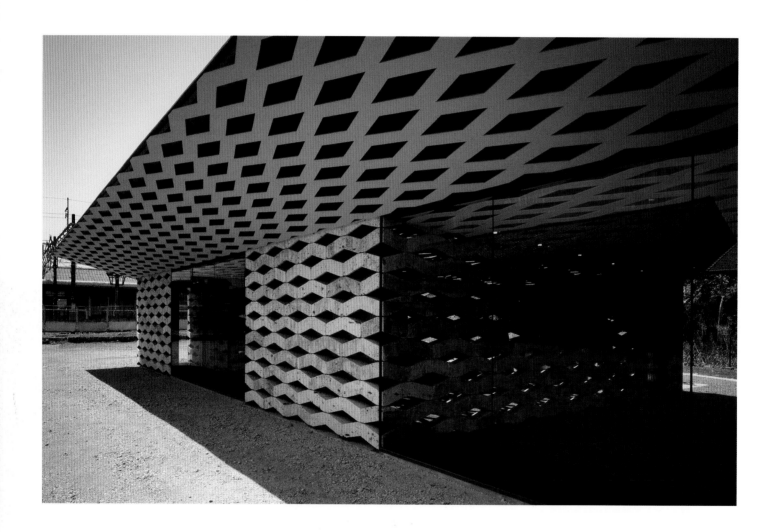

above
Exterior view of the shelter

opposite
**An entrance between two lacy
stone walls**

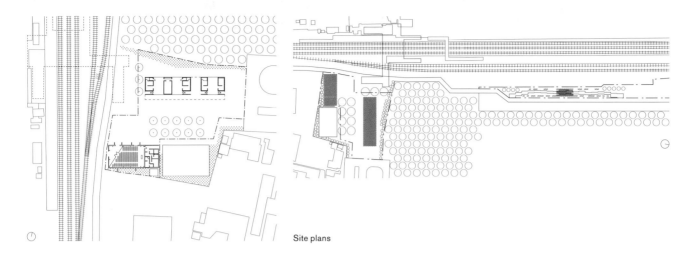

Site plans

The Chokkura Plaza and Shelter is a collection of single-story public facilities flanking a main plaza, with a multi-purpose room and restrooms on one side and a cafe and shops on the other. Collectively, this is a visitor center that adjoins the JR Hoshakuji train station in Takanezawa, a small township north of Tokyo. This project is an example of Kuma's tendency to fully exploit the properties of a specific material—here, stone pervades the project structurally and aesthetically.

The project's primary material is the local Oya stone, a porous rock that is easily cut and sculpted. Kuma notes that this kind of stone is an unusual material that possesses nearly the softness of soil and the lightness of air. Consequently, Chokkura Plaza and Shelter represents the evolution of the Oya stone from its solid state into an architecturally porous surface. Because Oya stone is fragile on its own, it was necessary to couple it with steel plates for added tensile strength. The plates are bent with slightly increasing angles to allow for progressively larger openings between the stone courses. The walls are both steel structure and load-bearing stone. The resulting screen filters light and views into the spaces. By night the diamond-shaped gaps glow in recognizable formation. The graphic quality of this combination is the structure, and vice versa. In other words, the material is the architecture.

Located roughly 328 feet (one hundred meters) from the plaza and main buildings, a park provides the grounds for the Green Shelter. This is an architectural folly composed of steel mesh boxes and reinforced with stainless-steel bars. While the shelter is currently devoid of other materials, it serves as the framework over which trumpet honeysuckle will grow in a thick, natural cover.

below
**Views from southwest (left)
and southeast (right)**

opposite, top
Frontal view from the south

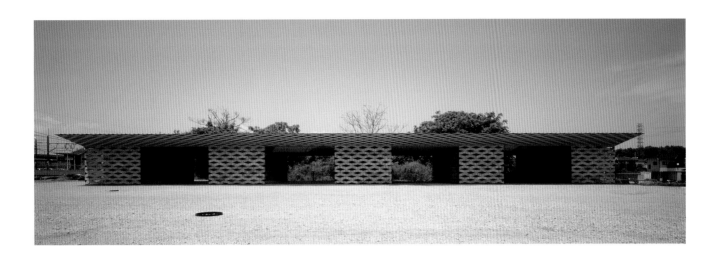

North elevation

South elevation

East elevation   West elevation

Longitudinal section

Cross section

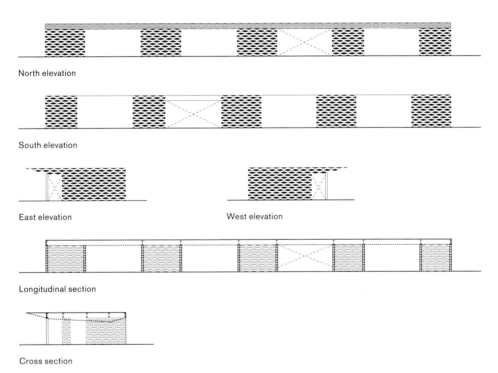

roof galvanium roofing sheet t0.4
rigid thermal insulation t25
asphalt roofing t1.0
wood chip cement board t18

galvanium plate t=1.2 SOP
steel angle: 100x75
soffit: silica calcium board t10

rainwater gutter
gutter: SUS t0.4

H-200x100x5.5x8

UB 200x200x8x12 paint in colour
1/100

H-200x200x8x12
PB t=1.2 AEP

2640
2040
450 150

external cladding: Oya stone
drain SUSE"105

wall: Lume Wall
(hollow section
polycarbonate sheet t40)

Steel Plate

plywood t24

silica calcium board t8
asphalt roofing
waterproof plywood t9

ceiling: silica calcium board t10

hollow section
polycarbonate sheet t40

external cladding: tuff stone
(reuse of existing material)

steel plate

glued chaff sheet t20
asphalt coating
crushed stone

under beam FL+2906

glued craftsheet t=20

1740   2410   2610   1740
8500

Detailed section of multipurpose exhibition hall

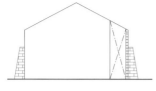

East elevation

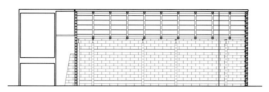

North elevation

Longitudinal section

West elevation   Section

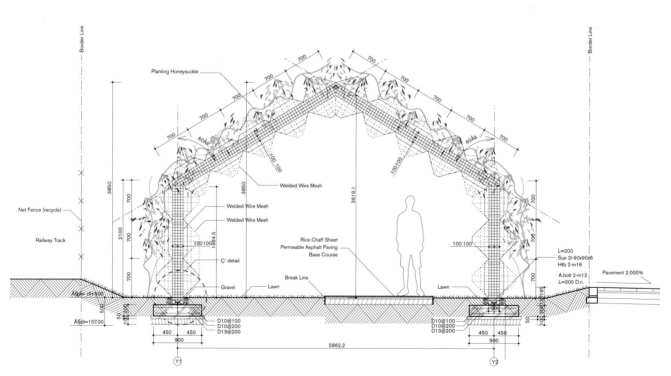

Detailed section of the stainless-steel-mesh green shelter

opposite, top
Interior and exterior views of the green shelter

opposite, bottom left
North facade of the renovated old storehouse

opposite. middle
Stone wall detail of the renovated old storehouse

opposite, bottom right
View of top-lit interior space

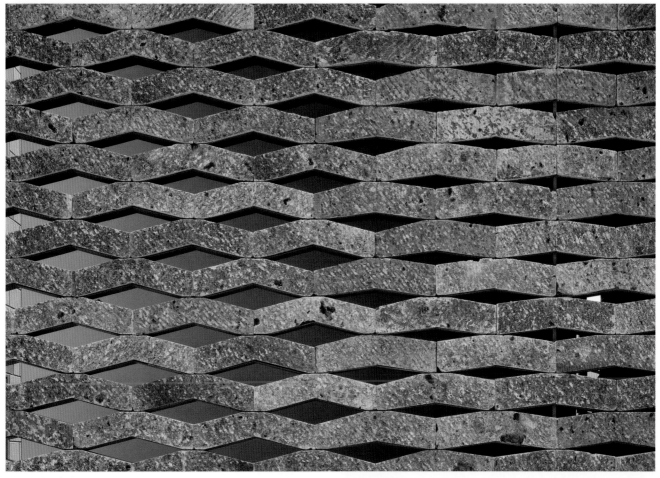

CHOKKURA PLAZA AND SHELTER   147

above
View of an unpaved passageway

opposite
Detail of the porous Oya-stone wall

Suntory Museum

Minato-ku, Tokyo
2004–7

above
View of the third-floor entrance lobby

opposite, top
**Main stairway connecting the third
and fourth floors**

opposite, bottom
**Upward view of the building's high
entry space**

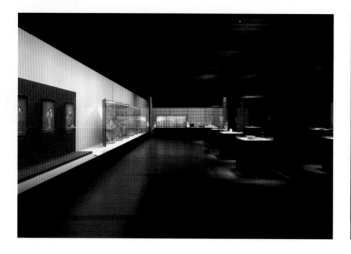 

Tokyo's popular Roppongi district, well known for its fashionable shops, bustling streets, and active nightlife, is the urban milieu for the Suntory Museum. The project is part of an agglomeration of shops, restaurants, offices, and a hotel called Tokyo Midtown—a collaborative effort between Skidmore, Owings & Merrill; Nikken Sekkei; and Kengo Kuma & Associates. As the main cultural addition to the district, the museum regularly displays traditional and modern Japanese arts and prints, along with rotating international exhibitions.

Kuma envisioned a calm, relaxed interpretation of the contemporary art museum, with a decidedly Japanese influence. From the outside, the museum sets itself apart from the Midtown block, with its vertical black-and-white striations of thin aluminum-reinforced ceramic panels. Inside, the museum offers what Kuma describes as a quiet, comfortable Japanese-style room, offering a space of socialization and leisure as a means to enjoy the displays. The main gallery is also the project's living room,

an airy double-height space that, depending on the exhibition, is sometimes brightly lit. The neighboring park is on display alongside the artwork, with large louvers softening the light and the view over the course of the day. Throughout the museum, human-friendly materials such as paulownia hardwood (for humidity control), and backlit washi-covered glass panels lend warmth to the galleries.

Although the building is composed of six floors and three basements, the public areas of the museum occupy only the third and fourth floors. The third-floor entry opens onto the atrium of an attached Midtown shopping mall, with a shop, cafe, and several galleries completing the arrangement. The level above is all gallery space, and a prominent glass-and-wood staircase connects the two levels, with views of the park unfolding in the background. The sixth floor is reserved for members of the museum, who have access to a terraced lounge and a tearoom, among other amenities.

top
Views of the fourth-floor
exhibition hall

right
Exterior views of the west
facade

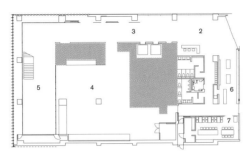

Third-floor plan

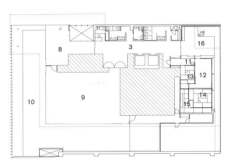

Sixth-floor plan

First-floor plan

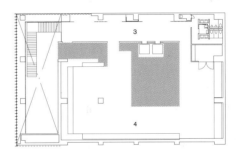

Fourth-floor plan

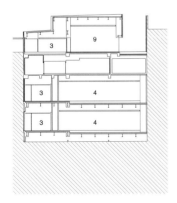

North section

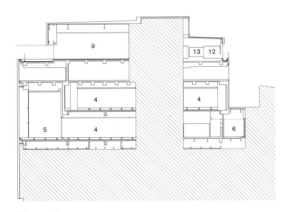

West section

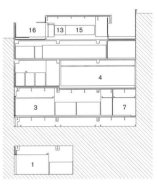

South section

top, from left
**Third-floor entrance lobby; cafeteria;
and sixth-floor Japanese garden**

1	Entrance	9	Hall
2	Main entrance	10	Deck
3	Lobby	11	Roji
4	Gallery	12	Ryuueri tearoom
5	Gallery void	13	Small tearoom
6	Shop	14	Big tearoom
7	Cafe	15	Mizuya
8	Members salon	16	Tearoom terrace

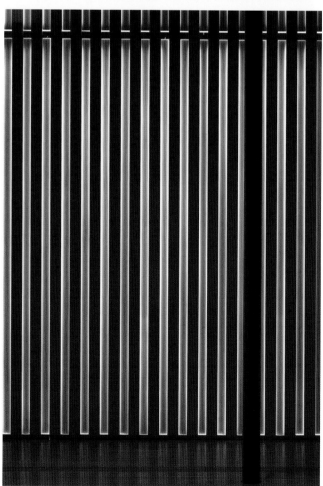

opposite, top
**View of the double-story gallery with
vertical louvers open**

opposite, bottom left
View of the gallery with louvers closed

opposite, bottom right
Detail of closed louvers

above
**Interior view of Japanese-style room
on the sixth floor**

Shiseikan, Kyoto University of Art and Design

Sakyo-ku, Kyoto
2005–8

above
Exterior view from the northwest

opposite
**Detail of the vertical stone louvers
on the west facade**

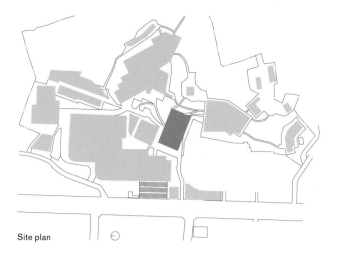

Site plan

Kyoto University of Art and Design commissioned the Shiseikan facility, or Student Union Hall, to accommodate the growing need for additional studio space and lecture rooms. The project provides these and additional spaces for socializing within a boxlike volume of four stories and two basements. The building adjoins the university's steep hillside site, emerging from and hovering above the terrain.

The box is unconventional, however; it is clad in a dark steel skin and seems to thrust outward from the canted terrain. Its matte surface and angular geometry makes the volume appear as if hewn from the hillside rock. Parts of the rectangular block have been cut away to make way for entries or views, while a sloping rooftop garden transitions into the natural slope of the site. A cascading set of stairs leads down to the main campus level and provides an entrance to the building. Oversized stone louvers anchor the project on two sides, simultaneously acting as structure, abstract ornament, and shade.

A stepped plaza sits beneath the building, providing students with a sheltered, open-air place for socializing or informal school gatherings. It also offers a more direct route to some lecture rooms and studios. The university's newest cafeteria and dining hall, characterized by broad square windows and exposed fluorescent lighting, occupy the top floor, and a small group of lecture rooms at the apex of the building open onto the roof garden.

Roof-level plan

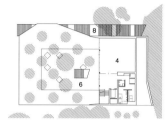

Fourth-floor plan

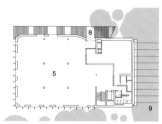

Third-floor plan

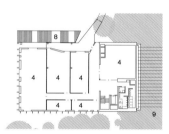

Second-floor plan

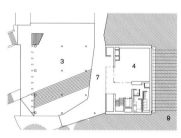

First-floor plan

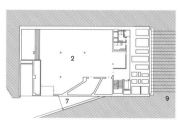

Basement level-one plan

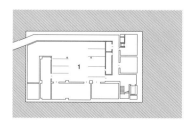

Basement level-two plan

West elevation

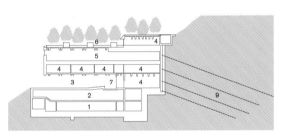

Longitudinal section

South elevation

1 Parking
2 Studio
3 Students' free space
4 Lecture room
5 Cafeteria
6 Rooftop garden
7 Ramp
8 Stair
9 Earth anchor

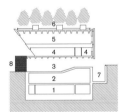

Cross section

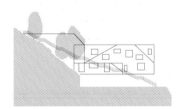

North elevation

top
**Views of the landscaped
rooftop terrace**

right
Third-floor entrance lobby

above
Views of the north facade

opposite
**Exterior stairway under the slanting
north facade**

above
Detail of the stone louvers

opposite, top
**Interior view of second-floor
entrance**

opposite, bottom
Third-floor study and meeting hall

NEW MATERIALS

INNOVATIVE BUILDING ENVELOPES

LVMH

—

Chuo-ku, Osaka
2002–4

above
**Daytime and evening views,
from the northwest**

opposite
**Detail of the glass-and-stone
west facade**

Inhabiting a prominently visible site along Osaka's busy Midosuji thoroughfare, this mid-rise building houses one of Louis Vuitton Japan Group's branches. This mixed-use project contains offices and several of the company's boutiques, and was envisioned as a glowing stone box.

The facade features two distinct material treatments, which approximately reflect the use of the building's interior spaces. The first cladding type is for the offices on floors three through seven, and it is displayed on the building as colored stone and glass. This facade system uses two types of panels. The first is made of 0.16-inch-thick (four-millimeter) translucent onyx from Pakistan, sandwiched between glass plates. The second, more transparent panel has a sheet of polyethylene terephthalate (PET) film with a printed pattern approximating that of the onyx between the same glass plates.

Shops occupy the first two floors and basement, and an access corridor serves as the spine for supporting spaces at the back of the L-shaped site, along with accommodating elevator cores for primary circulation. This arrangement is consistent throughout the building's nine floors. An event space occupies the roof and provides open-air room for hosting private engagements.

top, left
Interior of lobby on a general office floor

top, right
Interior of an office

below
Daytime and evening views of the rooftop terrace

Basement level-one plan

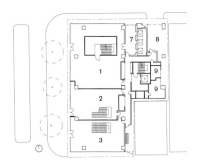

First-floor plan

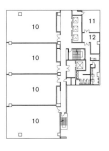

Second- to eighth-floor plan

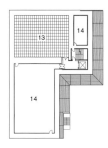

Roof plan

1 Shop A
2 Shop B
3 Shop C
4 Parking
5 Pump room
6 Disaster control room
7 EV hall
8 Parking
9 Garbage collection spot
10 Office
11 Outdoor machine space
12 Machine room
13 Event space
14 Roof floor machine space

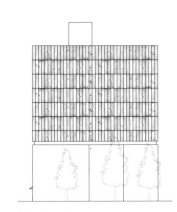

West elevation

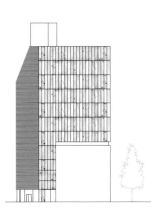

North elevation

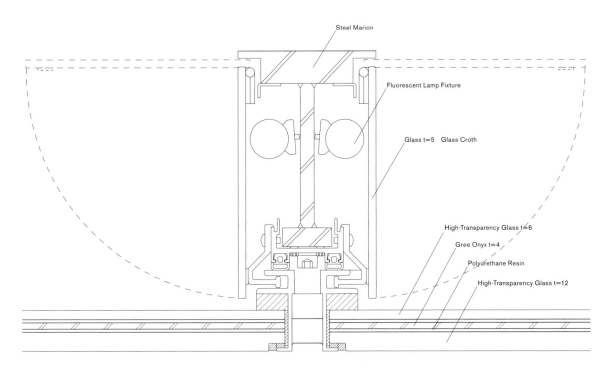

Steel Marion

Fluorescent Lamp Fixture

Glass t=5   Glass Croth

High-Transparency Glass t=6

Gree Onyx t=4

Polyurethane Resin

High-Transparency Glass t=12

Structural facade detail

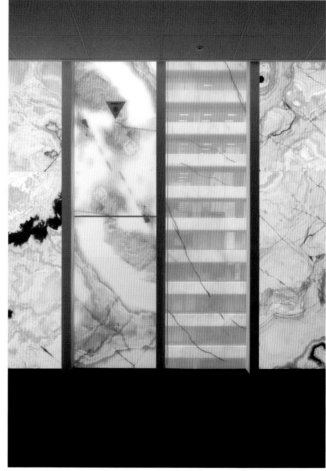

above, left
Entrance to the building

above, right
Interior view of the glass-and-stone facade

opposite, top
First-floor lobby

opposite, bottom
Interior detail of the facade

Fukuzaki Hanging Garden

Minato-ku, Osaka
2003–5

above
Evening view from the southeast

opposite
Detail of the south facade

 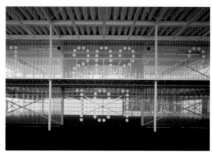 

A community facility with multifunction rooms and play spaces for children, this temporary structure is designed to last only ten years. The building sits at the corner of a large block in Osaka's Minato ward, an area that borders industrial and residential zones. As a result, the project's surrounding neighborhood contains storage warehouses and a golf driving range.

This project is an exploration of the idea of "weak architecture," which in this case manifests through the softness of the primary material. The entire front facade and numerous interior surfaces are composed of vertical strips of bright orange vinyl, a material commonly used in factories and for various manufacturing processes. The overlapping pieces are fastened together using flat bolts and stiffened with cables. This soft, flexible system absorbs the impact of the children at play and also withstands strong winds. Functionally, the vinyl forms the spatial enclosure, but gaps between the pieces allow the interior spaces to breathe.

Since the project does not have normal heating and air-conditioning requirements, the slab of the upper level could be reduced to minimum dimensions: two 0.35-inch (nine-millimeter) painted steel plates sandwich an iron grid, for a total thickness of 2.68 inches (6.8 centimeters). Bolts clamp the assembly here as well so that the building can be easily disassembled at the end of its use.

Behaving more as sheltered outside space than as a fully insulated enclosure, the project organizes its 5,939 square feet (552 square meters) of activity spaces around two levels. An interior plaza and large multifunction rooms make up the ground floor, which is paved with the same asphalt found outside of the pavilion. A ramp at the front of the building leads to the second floor, which houses three additional workrooms and an open gallery overlooking the play area.

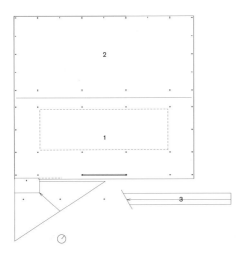

Ground-floor plan

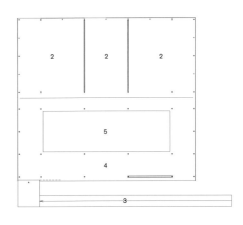

First-floor plan

1 Plaza
2 Workspace
3 Slope
4 Gallery
5 Void

Section

South elevation

East elevation

North elevation

West elevation

opposite, top
Views of the play space

opposite, bottom left
View from the south

opposite, bottom right
**The building in its surrounding
urban environment at dusk**

above
Evening view with the approaching ramp

opposite
Interior view showing mezzanine

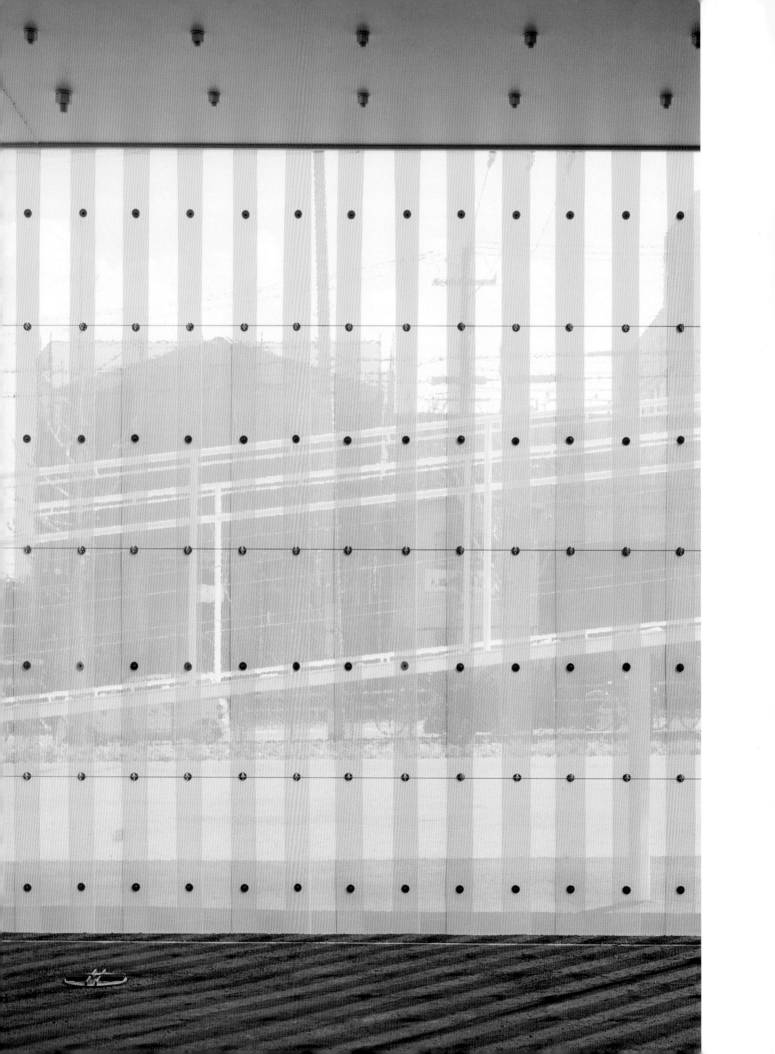

opposite
Interior detail of the south facade

above
View of the two-story play space

Z58 Zhongtai Box
—

Shanghai, China
2003–6

above
The building with the sidewalk

opposite
**View of the street facade with
rows of planted ivy**

This project is the new headquarters for Zhongtai, a well-known lighting company in Shanghai. It fuses nature with the traditional Chinese workplace, providing the company's employees with a relaxing atmosphere for design-related activities.

The project's carefully choreographed natural elements create a calm haven, away from the city's busy atmosphere. A facade of vegetation buffers the interior spaces from the outside world. This screen is planted with mirror-surfaced stainless-steel planters, creating the illusion of doubling the green space. Behind this layer lies an airy, four-story atrium with a water basin and a wall constructed out of five thousand glass bars. With water running over the uneven surfaces, the wall becomes a threshold of white noise, through which one must pass in order to access the quietude of the spaces within. Kuma calls the vegetated screen and the glass waterfall "filters" that successively slow down city life to a more casual pace.

The project also reintroduces the homelike nature of the traditional Chinese work environment. Inside, the office's main showroom opens to the visitor. A sales lounge and offices, as well as a bar and cafe, are interspersed throughout ground level. The second and third floors contain a double-height office area, along with private offices, meeting rooms, and design rooms. A glass elevator connects these floors by way of the entry waterfall and glassy forecourt. This also leads to a series of guest pavilions at the top of the project, which includes a canteen lounge, kitchen, fitness area, and bathing and sauna facilities, all of which appear to float above the reflecting pool, with views expanding toward the surrounding city.

top, left
Interior of the fourth-floor lobby

top, middle and right
Views of the fourth-floor guest rooms

right
Remote view of building in its urban context

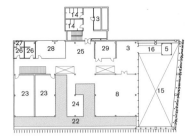

Fourth-floor plan

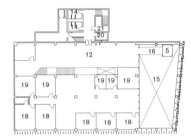

Third-floor plan

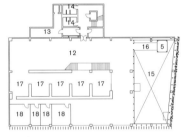

Second-floor plan

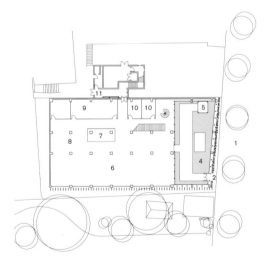

First-floor plan

1	Fangyu-road	16	EV bridge
2	Main entrance	17	Design room
3	Reception	18	Private office
4	Pool/atrium	19	Meeting room
5	Elevator	20	Coat room
6	Shop/showroom	21	Pantry
7	Bar	22	Pool
8	Cafe	23	Guest room
9	Sales lounge	24	Water lounge
10	Office/sales	25	Lounge/library
11	Staff entrance	26	Bath
12	Zongtai office	27	Sauna
13	Storage	28	Fitness
14	Bath staff	29	Kitchen
15	Void/atrium		

right, top
Fourth-floor lounge

right, bottom
**View of the entrance atrium, with
glass-covered wall and cascading water**

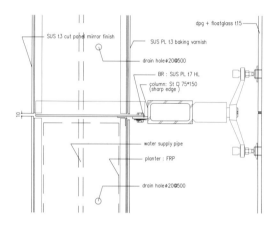

Elevation

Structural detail of east facade

SUS t3 cut panel mirror finish
SUS PL t3 baking varnish
dpg + floatglass t15
drain hole φ20@500
BR : SUS PL t7 HL
column: St □ 75*150 (sharp edge)
water supply pipe
planter : FRP
drain hole φ20@500
10

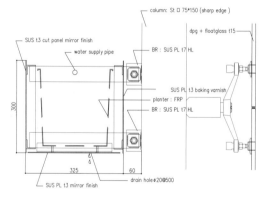

Elevation detail

300
500
300
500
300
2500

column: St □ 75*150 (sharp edge)
SUS t3 cut panel mirror finish
column: St □ 75*150 (sharp edge)

planter : FRP
SUS t3 cut panel mirror finish
dpg + floatglass t15
OUTSIDE
INSIDE

Close-up detail of east facade

column: St □ 75*150 (sharp edge)
dpg + floatglass t15
SUS t3 cut panel mirror finish
water supply pipe
BR : SUS PL t7 HL
SUS PL t3 baking varnish
planter : FRP
BR : SUS PL t7 HL
drain hole φ20@500
SUS PL t3 mirror finish
300
325
60

top, left
View of the entrance

top, right
Interior detail of the east facade

opposite
Close-up of the east facade

above
View of the fourth-floor lounge, "floating"
on a shallow pool of water

opposite
Entrance atrium viewed from the
fourth-floor bridge

Tiffany Ginza

—

Chuo-ku, Tokyo
2007–8

above
**Daytime and evening views along
Chuó-dóri avenue**

opposite
**Interior of the two-story entrance space
with reflective-glass wall panels**

Site plan

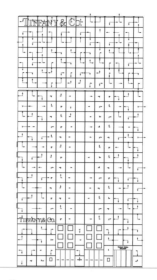

Elevation

For the renovation of Tiffany & Co.'s flagship store in Tokyo, Kuma constructed a completely new street facade and reconfigured the two main showrooms and guest lounge. The building is located at the heart of Ginza, one of Tokyo's most expensive shopping districts, well known for its couture boutiques.

The new facade is an elegantly abstract reference to the cutting technique used to facet precious stones, as well as the simplicity of the renowned Tiffany setting. The building's only elevation consists of numerous custom-made glass panels—each composed of a layer of aluminum honeycomb sandwiched between two sheets of glass—arrayed at random angles to catch and reflect light. The angles and textures produce ever-changing results depending on weather and the time of day. In essence, the architecture carries the Tiffany brand to the degree that literal signage is no longer required.

The interior spaces are finished with a broad array of luxurious materials. Visitors entering a two-story entrance hall, heightened by its mirrored ceiling, are greeted with an illuminated showcase wall of translucent stone and transparent display boxes. Vertical strips of wood, lit softly from above, line the walls, leading the visitor up to the second level. Marking the exclusive guest lounge and sales area on the third floor is a chandelier of flattened acrylic boxes and aluminum honeycomb.

Third-floor plan

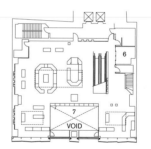

Second-floor plan

1 Back office area
2 Restroom
3 Customer service
4 Chandelier
5 Guest lounge
6 Private sales
7 Feature wall (crystal stone)

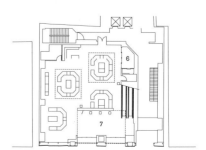

First-floor plan

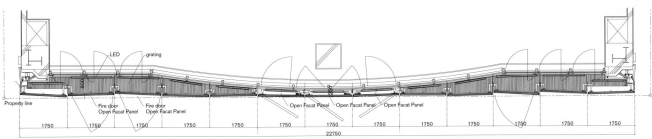

LED   grating

Property line

Fire door
Open Facat Panel

Fire door
Open Facat Panel

Open Facat Panel   Open Facat Panel   Open Facat Panel

1750   1750   1750   1750   1750   1750   1750   1750   1750   1750   1750   1750   1750

22750

Curtain-wall plan

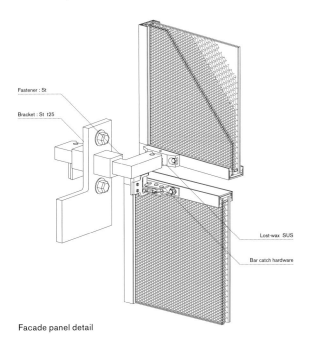

Fastener : St

Bracket : St t25

Lost-wax SUS

Bar catch hardware

Facade panel detail

top
**Detail of the front facade of special glass
panels attached at various angles**

right
**Interior view of the laminated double-glass
and aluminum honeycomb screens**

opposite
Chandelier of acrylic panels with sandwiched-aluminum honeycomb on the third floor

above
View of second-level sales floor

Opposite House Hotel

—

Beijing, China
2005–8

above
Exterior view from the southwest

opposite
**Interior of the central atrium, with suspended
drape of metal fabric**

Opposite House Hotel is located in the northern half of a new Beijing development called Sanlitun Village. The hotel occupies the southeastern corner of the block, planned by Kengo Kuma and Associates, which also includes buildings by SHoP Architects, LOT-EK, and Beijing Matsubara and Architects. Both the Sanlitun North block and the hotel refer to a traditional Chinese siheyuan courtyard formation. Along with the hotel, the buildings enclose a central courtyard with a sunken garden and four small commercial pavilions also designed by Kuma.

Despite having 154,225 square feet (14,328 square meters) allocated over six floors and two basements, the Opposite House Hotel maintains a human scale by avoiding the use of large, unbroken surfaces on the rectangular volume. The material expression of the hotel's facades mutates in accordance with changing light conditions, with panels of variegated glass modulating the elevations in a near-random manner. The materials appear pixelated, yet they retain strong connections with the region's graphic tradition, as silk-screened ceramics deploy patterns based on traditional Chinese lattice screens.

Upon entering, visitors are greeted by an assortment of restaurants and bars—each with a distinct visual and material theme. The ground-level arrangement flows freely around a central gallery, an atrium with reflecting pools, and diaphanous draped metal fabric. The atrium overlooks an eighty-two-foot (twenty-five-meter) swimming pool on the level below. Fiber-optic lighting hovers above the water, adding to the low-lit glow. This lower level also contains the hotel's other fitness amenities, including an exercise room and a juice bar. Additionally, the atrium provides the focus for the ninety-nine guest rooms above, which are arrayed around the central space. Low atrium balustrades, finished with reflective red acrylic panels, play against the rougher wood featured in the corridors. The "studio" rooms—with four distinct types and a two-level penthouse—are characterized by clean lines, reserved but warm materials, and ample natural light.

top, left
**First-floor reception shaped
as large display of acrylic "boxes"**

top, middle and right
Interior views of guest rooms

opposite, top
**View of north facade and sunken
courtyard**

opposite, middle
View of south facade

opposite, bottom
Close-up of glass panel

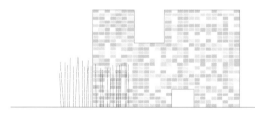

West elevation

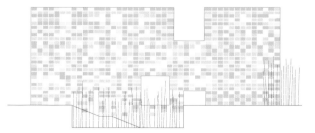

North elevation

Typical floor plan

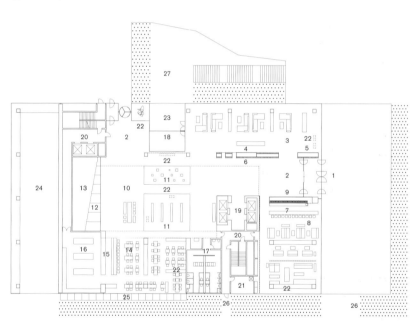

Ground-floor plan

1 Entrance	12 Slanted glass wall	
2 Vestibule	13 Open to swimming pool	23 Terrace
3 Reception	14 Cafe	24 Parking ramp
4 Staff work station	15 Espresso bar	25 Skylight
5 Luggage storage	16 Kitchen	26 Bamboo garden
6 Art display wall	17 Toilet	27 Sunken garden
7 Bar	18 Office	28 Atrium/mesh screen
8 Bar seating area	19 Elevator lobby	29 Guest room: Studio 45
9 Bar wine cellar	20 Service	30 Guest room: Studio 70
10 Atrium gallery	21 Mechanical room	31 Guest room: Studio 95
11 Reflecting pool	22 Art display	32 Hallway

above, left
**Woven-metal mesh screen in
the first-floor bar**

opposite, top
Interior view of the first-floor bar

above, right
**Entrance to the top-floor suite with
woven bamboo screens**

opposite, bottom
**Two-story-high space of the pool
on level B2**

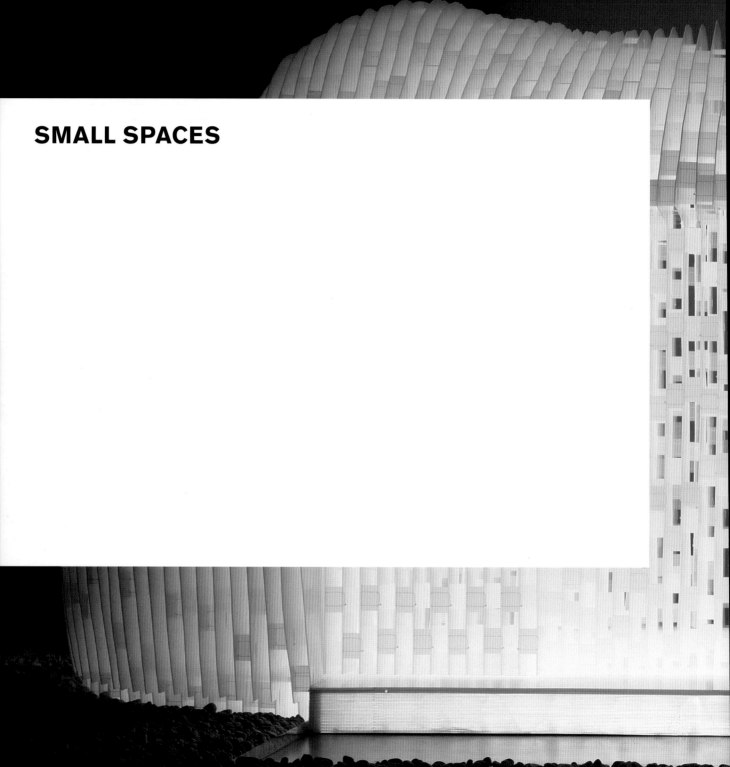

SMALL SPACES

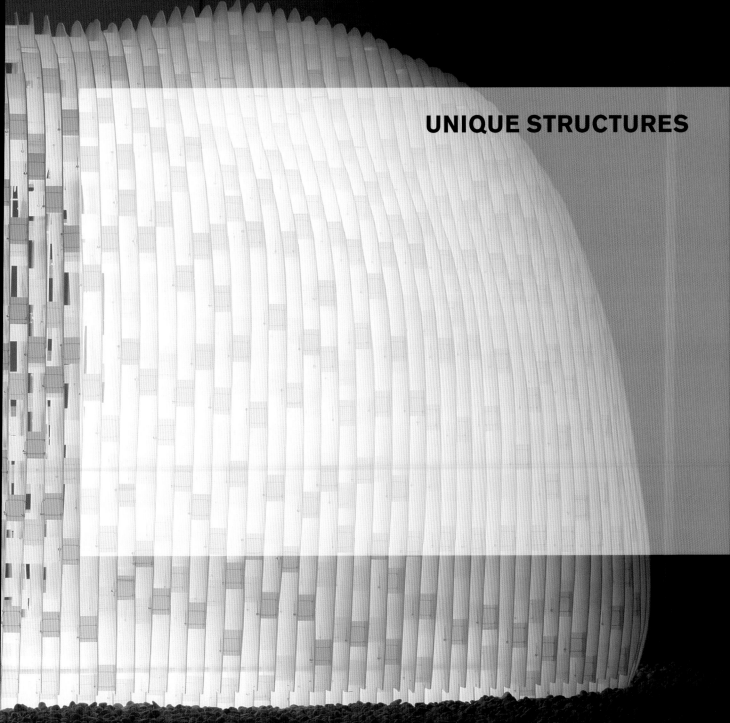

UNIQUE STRUCTURES

Paper Snake

—

Anyang, South Korea
2005–6

The Paper Snake is a public art installation that provides resting space within a forest. Part of the Anyang Public Art Project, this permanent construction offers areas from which to view the city, located on the outer reaches of Seoul, as well as the surrounding natural landscape.

The pavilion is formed out of a series of contiguous, angular planes that appear to fold and coil within the setting. These planes only partially enclose the space, thus implying zones for resting. Existing trees and the undulating topography govern the locations of these areas. Together with the pavilion, these elements frame ever-changing views of the surrounding scenery. While the visitor wanders through the terrain, pausing and gazing, the pavilion follows a similar meandering trajectory.

The distinctive planar form of the Paper Snake is due to the assembly of plastic and paper, and the pavilion deploys this set of materials in a singular, consistent fashion. With a total thinness of 1.85 inches (4.7 centimeters), the paper honeycomb works in tandem with sheets of fiber-reinforced plastic. The result is a membrane that is alternately transparent or solid, depending on one's approach to the pavilion or the angle of light as it plays against the planes. It is a porous screen that registers the shadows and colors of the landscape onto its surfaces throughout the course of the day.

right, top
Overall view of installation in the natural landscape

right, bottom
"Interior" of one of the shelters

opposite, from top
Exterior view; details of the honeycomb panels of plastic and paper

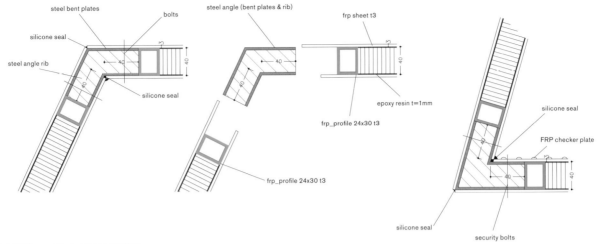

steel bent plates
bolts
silicone seal
steel angle (bent plates & rib)
frp sheet t3
steel angle rib
silicone seal
epoxy resin t=1mm
frp_profile 24x30 t3
frp_profile 24x30 t3
silicone seal
FRP checker plate
silicone seal
security bolts

Detail "A": panel-to-panel connections

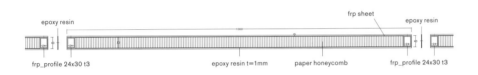

epoxy resin
frp sheet
epoxy resin
frp_profile 24x30 t3
epoxy resin t=1mm
paper honeycomb
frp_profile 24x30 t3

Detail "B": subpanel-to-subpanel connection

frp sheet t3
40
24
frp_profile 24x30 t3
epoxy resin t=1mm
paper honeycomb

Detail "C": side of panel

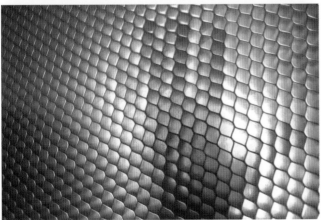

Elevation showing locations of
details "A," "B," and "C"

Oribe Teahouse

Tajimi, Gifu Prefecture
2005

The Oribe Teahouse installation explores temporary and portable assemblies as a new means of defining space. Based on the similarly amorphous ceremonial tea bowls by daimyo teamaster Furuta Oribe, this project is made of parallel layers of translucent, white-corrugated plastic normally used for postal shipping boxes. These layers make up the "ribs" of the project and the arbitrarily placed spacers. The pieces fasten together with standard plastic ties, allowing for easy disassembly into flat packages. The teahouse appears to be either solid or transparent, depending on the angle of approach. A backlit plastic floor enlivens the space with diffuse light.

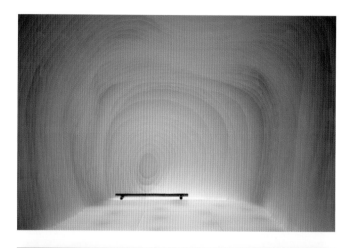

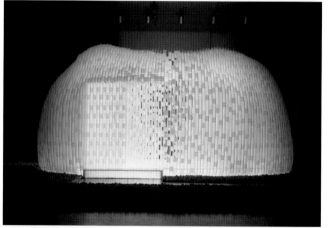

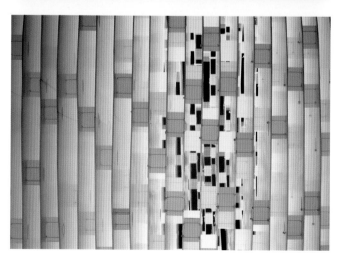

right, top
Interior view of the teahouse

right, middle
Exterior view of the structure illuminated from within

right, bottom
Detail of the layered, corrugated plastic sheets

opposite, bottom
View of the structure

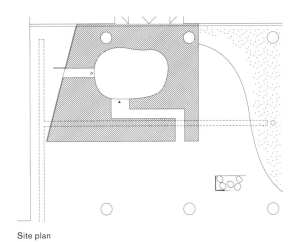

Site plan

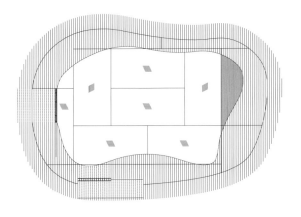

Plan diagram

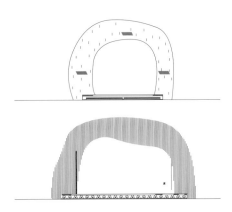

Section diagrams

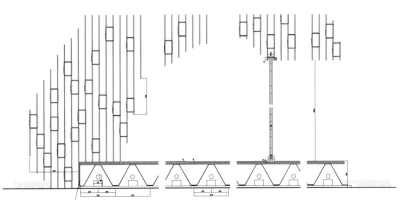

Section detail

KxK Pavilion, Hara Museum

Shinagawa-ku, Tokyo
2004–5

Created as an exhibition for an event hosted by a champagne maker, this forty-three-square-foot (four-square-meter) pavilion explores the intersection of new materials and portability. Here, materials transform the architecture into a soft, flexible, and dynamic organism. Interweaving a framework of ethylene vinyl acetate sheets made of a 0.8-inch (two-millimeter) resin cord and 0.8-inch (two-millimeter) shape-memory alloy rings, the ovoid form reacts to ambient temperatures and deforms accordingly. Kuma likens the effect to biological processes rather than to conventional architecture. When cooled, the shape-memory alloy rings lose rigidity, and the entire system collapses to enable compact packing.

right
Exterior views of the pavilion
illuminated at night

opposite
Detailed views of the translucent
membrane

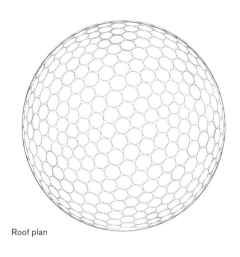

Roof plan

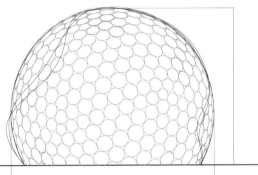
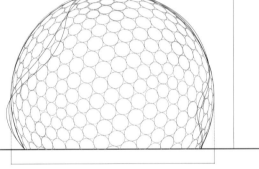

Elevation

Detail of elevation

Diagrams of transformation

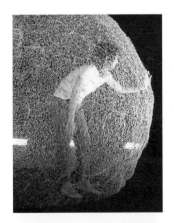

Modern Teehaus

Frankfurt, Germany
2005–7

Within this teahouse, Kuma merged his notions of "defeated architecture" with "breathing architecture" by actively and physically engaging the installation's environment. Its inflated form consists of a double-membrane skin made of Gore Tenara fabric. Unlike other membrane fabrics, Tenara contains no glass fibers, making it soft and light. It expands and contracts with air pressure and temperature, appearing almost to breathe. The material is waterproof and tear-resistant, and it transmits a high amount of light, up to 40 percent. Polyester strings hold the two membranes together, creating distinctive dimples on the teahouse's surfaces. Silhouettes of these connections, along with shadows and colors from the surrounding site, appear on the surfaces and project into the interior space. At night, LED lighting, concealed within the edges of the base, illuminates the membrane from within.

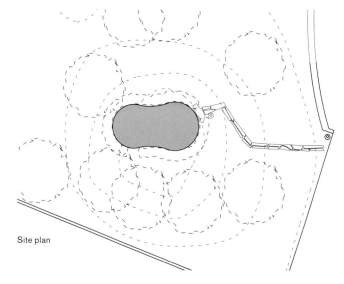

Site plan

right, top
Exterior view of the entrance

right, bottom
**Interior views with event
happening inside**

opposite
**Interior with folding partition and
tatami mats**

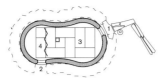

Ground-floor plan

Lower-level plan

1 Tea room entrance
2 Preparation room entrance
3 Tea room
4 Preparation room
5 Concrete basement

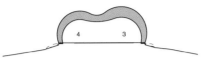

South section

West section

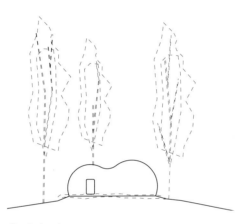

South elevation

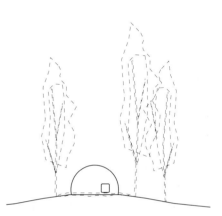

East elevation

Fuan Teahouse

Shizuoka, Shizuoka Prefecture
2007

Kuma describes the tea ceremony, along with the space in which it takes place, as a virtual realm, a kind of "device" that transports one from otherwise conventional surroundings. This is the basis for the Fuan Teahouse. In the installation, a thin translucent veil of super-organza material, weighing only eleven grams per square meter, was draped over a transparent vinyl-chloride helium balloon. Small stones anchor the cloth and balloon over an elevated tatami platform. There is no single, designated entry into the ceremonial space; instead, the fabric is lifted to allow entry. The entire system underscores its own material lightness; the slightest changes in airflow cause the fabric to sway and shimmer. Guests can feel this air passing through the fabric and the space. The ceremony brings participants into a new state of consciousness, and the teahouse establishes its form through an ephemeral approach to physical boundaries and materials.

While the project was initially conceived as a space for tea ceremonies, its simplicity and indeterminate nature make it suitable other uses as well. The Fuan Teahouse was first deployed as an installation at the World Tea Festival, held in Shizuoka, Japan, in November 2007. The concept was later broadened into a series of fabric-covered levitating balloons for experimental living, and exhibited at the Living Design Fair in Seoul, Korea, in 2008. In this latter version, a different use was assigned to each translucent "room," and the project exploited flexibility and material ambiguity as a new means for defining space.

right, top
Teahouse on display in the exhibition space

opposite, top
Overall view of the installation

opposite, bottom
Views of the super-organza veil

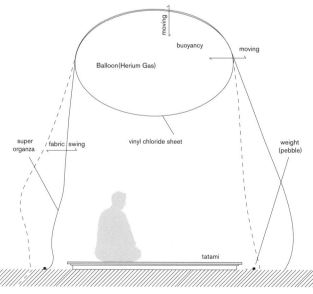

Section diagram

Casa Umbrella

—

Milan, Italy
2008

The Casa Umbrella exhibited as a temporary shelter prototype at the 2008 Milan Triennale. The project consisted of fifteen large custom-designed umbrellas, with covers made of DuPont Tyvek, a breathable, nonwoven polyester fabric commonly used for weather and moisture protection in construction applications. The umbrellas were assembled into an icosahedron. Zippered flaps linked them together, while the umbrellas' frames provided the structure. These were then fastened with ties typically used for diving suits. With simple assembly, the Casa Umbrella repurposed off-the-shelf products to create an ordinary application, but in a new combination.

above
Entrance to the shelter

right, from top
**Views of the pavilion under construction
and upon completion**

opposite, top
View from the southest corner

opposite, bottom
View with umbrella

Cidori

Milan, Italy
2007

Cidori was part of the 100 Years of Mondadori Capitale del Design exhibition held at Milan's Castello Sforzesco in 2007. The installation's name translates roughly as "one thousand birds," and it was made of numerous thin wooden elements assembled into an inverted nestlike structure. The pavilion made use of only this one material, with no nails, fasteners, or adhesives. A special notching technique was employed to interlock the pieces and to form a stable, sturdy, and visually transparent lattice framework. The project was lit from below in dramatic fashion to emphasize the end result. While this is a singular example, the project holds promise for further iterations and applications.

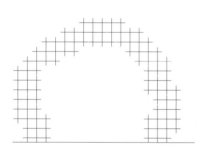
Section

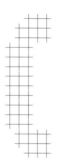
Floor plan

Diagram of the wooden elements

right
Detail of the pavilion in the evening

opposite, top
Detail of the wooden assembly

opposite, bottom
View of the pavilion in the courtyard of Castellon Sforzesco

URBAN-SCALE PROJECTS

SHAPING PUBLIC PLACES

Nagasaki Prefectural Art Museum

Nagasaki, Nagasaki Prefecture
2001–5

above
**Evening view from the north, with the
small canal crossing the site**

opposite, top
Detail of the west facade

opposite, bottom
View of the top-lit interior patio

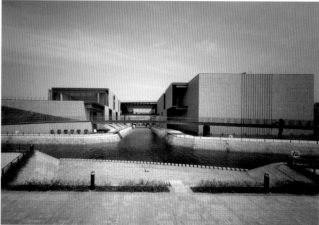

This major museum houses a large collection of artwork and artifacts, many dating back to an era, during the Edo period (1603–1868), that saw Nagasaki as one of Japan's only points of contact with the outside world. The project is located on a landfill site on the Port of Nagasaki, and it is bounded on the remaining three edges by busy roads. A canal bisects the museum, and pedestrian promenades hug both banks, putting the water's tidal fluctuations on full display to the public. The walkway also provides a viewing area for looking into the museum and therefore acts as an outdoor municipal exhibition space, drawing the city into the museum. The canal literally and figuratively immerses the museum within the site.

The experience of visiting the museum is affected by the site's strong intersection of urban characteristics, as well as by the natural landscape. At ground level, a broad plaza with a "river amphitheater" seeps toward one side of the museum and expands into the lofty entrance lobby. Much of the public program is located at this level, including a media center and a gallery facing the canal. The ground level in the other volume includes a narrowly proportioned, glass-enclosed "river gallery," as well as archives, stacks, and an information lab.

Exhibition halls and smaller galleries occupy the upper level; a wide glass bridge, acting doubly as the museum cafe, connects the two sides at this level. Occasional light wells and picture windows punctuate the spaces of the artist studios, offering glimpses of the city. Even the roof of the museum, including the upper surface of the bridge, is designed as a landscaped area for viewing the expansive panorama of the port city.

From a distance, the museum appears as screens of thin stone, metal, and glass. Vertical louvers composed of approximately 129,167 square feet (12,000 square meters) of Brazilian granite surround it. The louvers and the museum's primary enclosure do not always coincide, instead leaving partially enclosed outdoor spaces that are evocative of the traditional Japanese veranda.

above, left
Aerial view of the museum in its urban context beside Nagasaki Bay

above, right
View from the south

right
View of the citizens' arcade; interior view of the connecting bridge, with the cafe over the canal

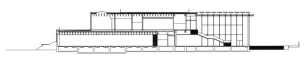

East-west section

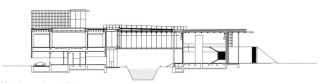

North-south section

East-west section

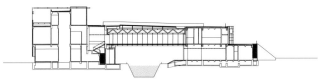

North-south section

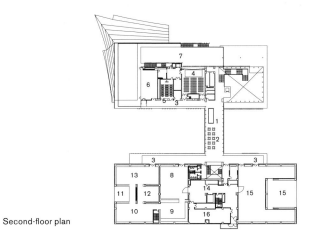

Second-floor plan

1 Bridge corridor
2 Cafe
3 Corridor
4 Atelier
5 Lecture room
6 Museum hall
7 Roof garden
8 Collection gallery one
9 Collection gallery two
10 Collection gallery three
11 Patio
12 Collection gallery four
13 Collection gallery five
14 Store house
15 Temporary gallery
16 Machine room

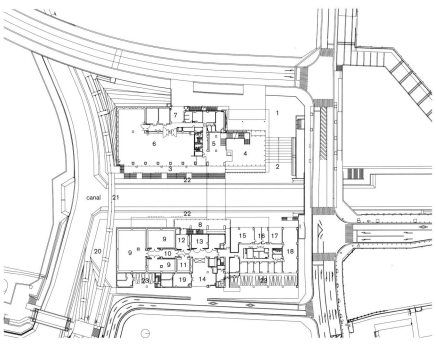

Site and first-floor plan

1 Gate plaza
2 Canal-side plaza
3 Canal-side corridor
4 Entrance
5 Reference desk
6 Public gallery
7 Loading dock one
8 Canal-side lobby
9 Storage
10 Storage anteroom
11 Temporary storage
12 Conservation room
13 Photo studio
14 Loading dock two
15 Office
16 Director's office
17 Meeting room
18 Study room
19 Machine room
20 Pool
21 Pedestrian bridge
22 Pedestrian
23 Private parking

opposite, top
View of the canal, from the north

opposite, bottom
Evening view of the canal, from the south

top
**Interior of the entrance lobby, looking west
toward Nagasaki Bay**

bottom
Second-floor passage overlooking the canal

above
**Interior of the entrance hall in the
gallery wing**

opposite
**View from the museum wing, looking
toward the gallery wing**

Tobata C Block

Kitakyushu, Fukuoka Prefecture
2005–7

above
**Aerial view of the entire complex,
from the west**

opposite
**Close-up view of the stepped-platform
arrangement overlooking the park**

Located in the southern city of Kitakyushu, the Tobata C Block is a mixed-use civic facility that includes the new local ward office, a welfare institution, a nursery, and private and public housing. The complex occupies a site in a dense residential neighborhood and introduces a range of facilities to revitalize the area.

Tobata C Block features undulating topography, and the combination of a landscaped base with tower structures above prefigures the much larger, subsequent development of Sanlitun SOHO. Tobata C Block specifies the experiential character of its various functions by means of landscaping techniques. With abundant curved lines suggestive of fluidity, the surface provides a scalar transition between the tall preexisting buildings on one side of the site and the cascading stepped-down seating looking toward the park on the other side. This theatrical urban gesture provides connections to the nursery playground as well as the semipublic garden shared by residents. Extensive use of natural materials enhances the organic quality of the project.

The larger facilities inhabit the areas beneath the landscape, where one can find the ward office and an activity center for handicapped persons, along with parking. The stepped surface of the landscape provides seating for the activities above, but those same steps offer shade for the ward office beneath. Privately owned and rental apartments, elderly housing, and daycare facilities populate the landscape, with numerous connections to the levels below.

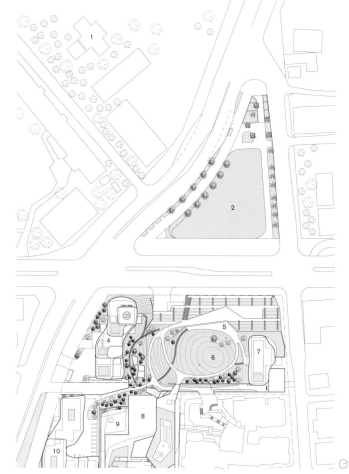

1 Shrine
2 Asoh park
3 Former ward office
4 Private housing complex
5 Tobata ward office
6 Park
7 Housing complex for the elderly
8 Senboh public nursery
9 Activity center for handicapped
   people
10 Public housing complex

top, left
View of the landscaped rooftop

top, middle and right
Interior views of the ward office

Site plan

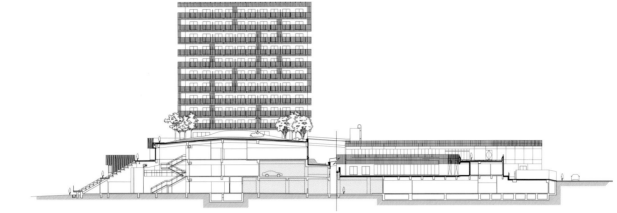

East-west section

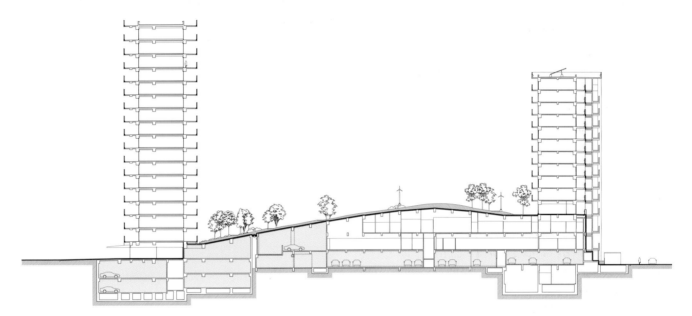

North-south section

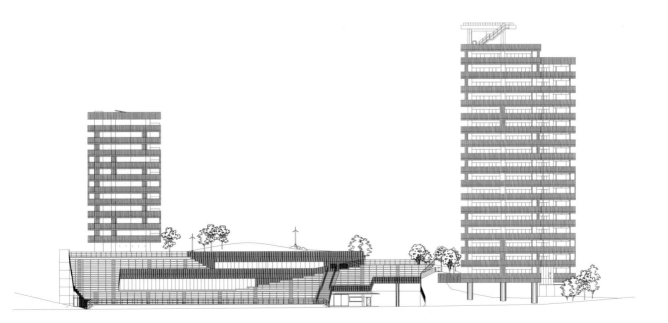

West elevation

above
**The layered and landscaped rooftops
of various public facilities**

opposite
Green park over the ward office

Asahi Broadcasting Corporation
Headquarters
———

Fukushima-ku, Osaka
2003–8

above
**Entrance hall behind the checkerboard
composite-wood-panel screen**

opposite
View of the complex, from the southeast

The Asahi Broadcasting Corporation Headquarters continues Kuma's exploration of the fusion of landscape with urban architecture as a means of producing new public spaces. This building provides studio space for one of Japan's primary news and broadcasting agencies. Overlooking the Dojima River, it is surrounded by the busy office district of Osaka.

The building consists of two rectangular blocks— a taller and a lower one—with an integrated landscape- like podium facing the river. Kuma explains that his intention was to open the otherwise closed entity to the city and to provide river-oriented spaces for all people, not just those associated with the company. The land- scaping enables the combination of private and public spaces. A set of two parklike terraces serve as viewing platforms for enjoying the view of the river: the upper, called Sky Terrace, provides employees with generous outdoor space on the tenth floor; and the lower one, the River Deck, rises from the river to form a podium and then makes its way back to the liveliness of the street on the other side of the building. Each of these is coupled with multistory open-air passages that frame the city of Osaka in the distance.

Various functions inhabit the tower's sixteen floors and basement, filling approximately 430,556 square feet (40,000 square meters). Offices make up much of the building, with much larger rooms distributed throughout its height. The base of the building houses the main

studios and parking, with commercial space lining the street. At the River Deck level, one can find the build- ing's flagship ABC Hall auditorium. On the tenth floor, an employee dining hall replete with a bar on the mezzanine level and a tearoom complement the Sky Terrace.

top, left
Aerial view of the building in its urban context, with the Dojima River in front

top, middle
View from across the river

top, right
The entrance hall in strong sunshine

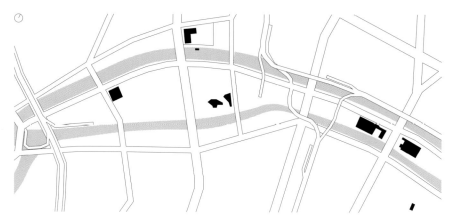

Site plan

Eleventh-floor plan   Twelfth-floor plan

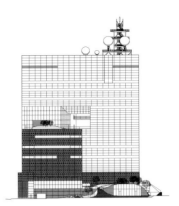

South elevation

Tenth-floor plan

East elevation

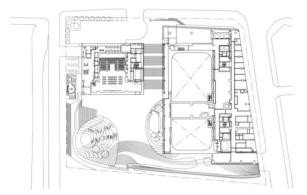

Third-floor plan

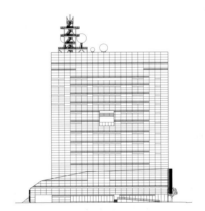

North elevation

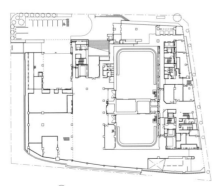

First-floor plan

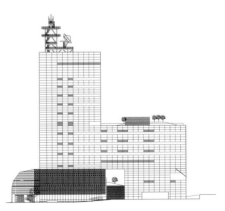

West elevation

above
**Interior stairway in the third-floor foyer
overlooking the river**

opposite, top
The landscaped "sky terrace"

opposite, bottom
The landscaped "river terrace"

opposite, top
Large public stairway

opposite, bottom
**Checkerboard screen viewed from the inside,
overlooking the public stairway**

above
Tenth-floor employee dining hall

Sanlitun Village South

—

Beijing, China
2005–7

above
View from the southeast

opposite
**Facade detail of the double-glazed panels
with multicolor prismatic acrylic**

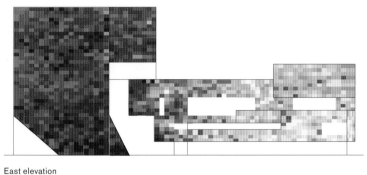

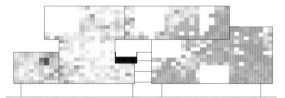

East elevation

North elevation

The south site of the Sanlitun Village project consists of a series of shopping and retail areas, as well as an event hall. It is an urban development, in which Kuma uses several ordinary but interconnected functions and building forms to shape new spaces for the city. Along with an additional building immediately to the north, the commercial building and the event hall define the four sides of a publicly accessible courtyard toward the middle of the block.

The shops are distributed between four primary floors in an approximate L-shaped configuration, while a taller tower rises at the site's southeast corner; all of which overlook the courtyard. Although the program is uniform, Kuma's design avoids the appearance of a monolithic shopping object by cutting paths into the overall volume, providing passages for shoppers and extending the activity of the city inward. This porosity provides views between clusters of shops, and the locations of these gaps differ from floor to floor. An array of thirty-five shades of prismatic acrylic

bars, sandwiched within double-glazed panels, reinforces the exterior's fragmented, pixelated character. With the tower located at the corner, the faceted facades and fluidity of space continue into the building as well: corners that appear to be cut away from the building volume give way to a lofty, multistory space, with mezzanine floors flying overhead. As a result, the experience of these shops is both varied and extroverted.

By comparison, the event hall is housed in a simpler volume with a trapezoidal plan; it is clad in translucent orange-colored glass-fiber-reinforced vinyl panels. As with the rest of the south site, it features a prominent spatial connection to the surrounding city. A double-height central hall opens toward either end of the building, with ample entrances connecting the street to the courtyard. Bars of supporting functions on two levels flank this central space, completing the volume. The roof featues an event space composed of broad, stepped seating that overlooks the entire development.

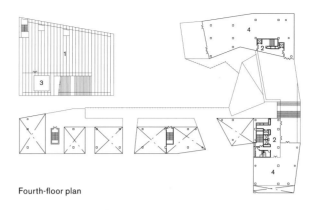

Fourth-floor plan

1 Event space
2 EV lobby
3 Mechanical space
4 Retail

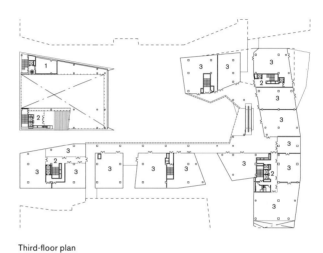

Third-floor plan

1 Mechanical room
2 EV lobby
3 Retail

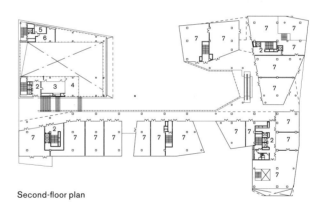

Second-floor plan

1 Gallery
2 EV lobby
3 Seminar room
4 VIP room
5 Administration
6 AV control
7 Retail

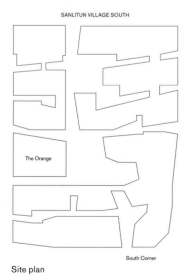

SANLITUN VILLAGE SOUTH

The Orange

South Corner

Site plan

opposite, left
**East facade of the shopping
block**

opposite, right
**View of the event hall from
the plaza**

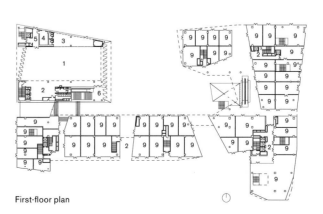

First-floor plan

1 Event hall
2 EV lobby
3 Storage/cloakroom
4 Fire control room
5 Service
6 Escalator lobby
7 WC
8 Storage
9 Retail

above, left
View of the east facade

above, right
View of the public plaza in the village

opposite
**View of the Uniqlo building through a
narrow pedestrian lane**

Sanlitun SOHO

—

Beijing, China
2007–10

above
Rendered view of complex, from the north

opposite
**View of the complex's north entrance, with
the undulating valley among buildings**

Kuma's recent foray into China includes very large-scale projects, often encompassing multiple buildings. Sanlitun SOHO—distinct from Sanlitun Village, of which the Opposite House Hotel is a part—is one such project. Situated in Beijing's Chaoyang District, the entire SOHO development encompasses more than 5 million square feet (465,500 square meters) of offices, retail space, and residential units. This multi-use enclave was designed as a rich urban atmosphere, akin to that of New York's own SoHo or Tokyo's Aoyama neighborhoods.

Regarding the complex's general organization, the first several levels form an amorphous undulating base and primarily house retail and commercial spaces. Along with the park and river landscape at ground level, this zone provides the development's active public strata. Above, each tower houses a single type of program, with residential towers interspersed between office towers.

While the project occupies a footprint of approximately 263,716 square feet (24,500 square meters), Kuma envisions it not as a monolithic volume, but instead as a collection of softened forms connected by hard landscaping, vegetation, and water. The project features a series of nine towers, ranging up to twenty-eight floors, that he describes as a "village of skyscrapers." Each has a unique footprint, while a mosaic-like facade strategy provides unity and local differentiation. The other significant connective device is a curvilinear valley, featuring water, bridges, and landscaping elements, and is lined with multiple levels of shops and amenities. Thus, the SOHO development offers experiential variety within a broad, cohesive framework.

top, left
View of the proposed water park

top, right
Detail of the B1-level promenade

opposite
The B1-level valley and interior views of the atrium on the lower level

1	Office A
2	Retail 1
3	Office B
4	Retail 2
5	Office C
6	Office D
7	Office E
8	Retail 3
9	Residential A
10	Residential B
11	Retail 4
12	Retail 5
13	Residential C
14	Residential D

Roof plan, also showing the site below

Biographical Notes and Awards

1954   Born in Kanagawa Prefecture, Japan

1979   Completed the master course, Department of Architecture, University of Tokyo

1985   Visiting scholar, Columbia University Graduate School of Architecture, Planning, and Preservation and the Asian Cultural Council

1987   Spatial Design Studio, founded

1990   Kengo Kuma and Associates, founded

1998   Professor, Faculty of Environmental Information, Keio University

2001   Professor, Faculty of Science and Technology, Keio University

2009   Professor, Graduate School of Architecture, University of Tokyo

AWARDS

1994   Good Design Architecture Award from the Japanese Ministry of International Trade and Industry: Yusuhara Visitor's Center

1995   Grand prize, JCD Design Award, cultural/public institutions: Kiro-san Observatory

1997   Architectural Institute of Japan Award: Noh Stage in the Forest; First place, AIA DuPONT Benedictus Award: Water/Glass; Grand prize, Regional Design Award: Yusuhara Visitor's Center

1999   Honorable mention, unbuilt architecture category, Boston Society of Architects

2000   Grand prize, Prize of AIJ, Tohoku chapter: River/Filter; Grand prize, INTER INTRA SPACE: Kitakami Canal Museum; Director General of Forestry Agency Prize: Ando Hiroshige Museum

2001   International Stone Architecture Award: Stone Museum; Tougo Murano Prize: Ando Hiroshige Museum

2002   Spirit of Nature Wood Architecture Award, Finnish Forest Foundation

2005   Marble Architecture Award: Nagasaki Prefectural Art Museum

2007   International Architecture Award, Best New Global Design, the Chicago Athenaeum, Museum of Architecture and Design: Chokkura Plaza and Shelter; Detail Prize, special prize: Chokkura Plaza and Shelter

2008   Energy Performance + Architecture Award: general body of work; Emirates Glass LEAF Award, public building: Suntory Museum

EXHIBITIONS

1992   Tokyo Columns, M2, Setagaya-ku, Tokyo (solo exhibition)

1993   City of Labyrinth, Sezon Museum of Art, Toshima-ku, Tokyo, Tsukashin Hall, Amagasaki, Hyogo Prefecture

1995   Velocity of Transmission, Gallery MA, Minato-ku, Tokyo (solo exhibition); Venice Biennale, Venice, Italy

1996   Milan Triennial, Milan, Italy

1997   Virtual Architecture, Museum of the University of Tokyo, Bunkyo-ku, Tokyo

2000   Venice Biennale, Venice, Italy; ARCHILAB, Orléans, France

2001   Japanese Avant Garde: Reality Projection, 16 Young Japanese Architects, Royal Institute of British Architects, London, Great Britain

2002   ARCHILAB, Orléans, France; Venice Biennale, Venice, Italy

2004   Takeo Paper Show: HAPTIC, Spiral Garden & Hall, Minato-ku, Tokyo; Venice Biennale, Venice, Italy

2004   New Trends of Architecture in Europe and Asia-Pacific, Lille, France; Kengo Kuma: Defeated Architecture, Matsuya Ginza, Chuo-ku, Tokyo (solo exhibition); NIWA: where the particle responses, Chiyoda-ku, Tokyo

2004   3_2_1 New architecture in Japan and Poland, Centre of Japanese Art and Technology, Manggha, Krakow, Poland; ARCHILAB, Mori Art Museum, Minato-ku, Tokyo

2005   Oribe Tea House, Mino Ceramics Park, Tajimi, Gifu; Kengo Kuma: The Architecture Between Tradition and Innovation (travelling solo exhibition); EXTREME EURASIA, Spiral Garden & Hall, Minato-ku, Tokyo; Kengo Kuma x Krug, Hara Museum, Tokyo; Kuma Mock-Ups, GA Gallery, Shibuya-ku, Tokyo (solo exhibition)

2006   GA International, GA Gallery, Shibuya-ku, Tokyo; ARCHILAB, Orléans, France

2007   100 years of Mondadori Milan Design Capitol: Decode Elements, Milan, Italy; Swarovski Crystal Palace, Milan, Italy; Tokyo Design Premio, Tokyo Designers Week; Tsunagu, Mitsui Fudosan Residential booth, Milan, Italy; Kengo Kuma Two Carps: Water/Land–Village/ Urban Phenomenology, the Barbara Cappochin Biennial International Architectural Exhibition

2008   Casa Umbrella, Milan Salone, Milan, Italy; Venice Biennale, Venice, Italy; Fabricating the Modern Dwelling, Museum of Modern Art, New York, New York, United States; Material Immaterial, I space Gallery, Chicago, Illinois, and Pratt Institute, Brooklyn, New York, United States

COMPETITIONS

1993   Second prize, Niigata City Performing Arts Center Competition, Niigata, Niigata Prefecture; Second prize, Abashiri Urban Planning Competition, Abashiri, Hokkaido Prefecture

1996   Honorable mention, Kansai-kan, National Diet Library Competition, Kyoto; Third prize, Proposal for the Nagaoka Culture Forum, design competition, Nagaoka, Niigata Prefecture

2001   Shortlisted for second phase, Managed Workspace, RIBA competition, Yorkshire, Great Britain

2002   First prize, Tokyo University of Agricultural, Exhibition Center Competition, Setagaya-ku, Tokyo; First prize, Mori Building Corporation, Odaiba Museum Competition, Minato-ku, Tokyo

2003   Honorable mention, San Jose University School of Art Museum, San Jose, California, United States; Shortlisted for final phase, the Hepworth Gallery, Wakefield, RIBA competition, Wakefield, Great Britain

2003   Shortlisted for second phase, European Central Bank Urban Planning and Architectural Design Competition, Frankfurt, Germany; Honorable Mention, Kuamgusu Minakata Research Center Competition, Tanabe, Wakayama Prefecture

2004   Shortlisted for final phase, National Palace Museum Southern Branch International Design Competition, Chiayi, Taiwan

2005   Shortlisted for International Competition for Museum of History of Polish Jews in Warsaw, Warsaw, Poland

2006   Shortlisted for a competition for Shanghai Natural History Museum, Shanghai, China; Finalist for BAM/PFA, Barkley Art Museum and Pacific Film Archive, Los Angeles, California, United States; Finalist, Barnes Foundation, Philadelphia, Pennsylvania, United States

2007   Architecture Competition for the Museum of Modern Art in Warsaw, Warsaw, Poland; First prize, Besancon City of Arts and Culture Architecture Competition, Besancon, France; First prize, Architectural competition for the complex of government buildings related to the area of the western railway station of Budapest, Hungary

2008   First prize, Granada Performing Arts Center Architectural Competition, Granada, Spain; First prize, International Invited Architectural Competition for iconic park and mixed development in Iskandar, Johor-Bahru, Malaysia; First prize, commercial and environmental design proposal for the Central Post Office, Tokyo, Japan; First prize, Asakusa Tourist Information Center Architectural Competition, Tokyo, Japan; Munch and Stenersen Museum Collections Competition, Oslo, Norway; Master Plan Competition for a New Thermal Complex, San Pellegrino Terme, Italy; Cologne Opera House Competition, Cologne, Germany; Courchevel Grandes Comber Site Development Project, Courchevel, France; Marseille Regional Foundation of Contemporary Art, Marseille, France; NHK Yamanashi Broadcasting Center, Tokyo, Japan; International Criminal Court, the Hague, the Netherlands; HafenCity Hamburg Zentrale Lage am Magdeburger Hafen, Hamburg, Germany

2009   First prize, Alibaba "Taobao City" Architectural Competition, Hangzhou, China; Basque Culinary Centre, Barcelona, Spain

Staff

TOKYO

Kengo Kuma
Minoru Yokoo
Toshio Yada
Akiko Shintsubo
Kenji Miyahara
Makoto Shirahama
Shuji Achiha
Teppei Fujiwara
Emiko Noguchi
Kazuhiko Miyazawa
Yuki Ikeguchi
Eishi Sakamoto
Shin Ohba
Hiroaki Akiyama
Tsuyoshi Kanda
Sayaka Mizuno
Masamichi Hirabayashi
Takumi Saikawa
Toshiki Meijo
Yoshihiro Kurita
Javier Villar Ruiz
Yuko Shimizu
Satoshi Adachi
Atsushi Kawanishi
Jumpei Matsushima
Suguru Watanabe
Takeyuki Saita
Tomokazu Hayakawa
Katinka Temme
Yuki Haba
Masao Tsuchiya
Tomoyuki Hasegawa
Hirofumi Yamada
Manami Kinjo
Jun Shibata
Hirokatsu Asano
Ryohei Tanaka

Tessei Suma
Ryota Torao
Diego Arahuetes Lopez
Nahoko Terakawa
Masafumi Harigai
Shuhei Kamiya
Ayumi Motose
Keiko Yoshida
Hiroaki Saito
Ritsuko Ameno
Balázs Bognár
Tomoko Sasaki
Mariko Inaba
Yoshihiko Seki
Tomotaka Kyo
Shinya Kojima
Keigo Yoshida
Marcin Sapeta
Makiko Sakai
Satoshi Onomichi
Shi Hu
Akio Saruta
Rika Hiratsuji
Hiroki Tominaga
Xinxuan Jiang
Omar Rabie
Shuhei Yamane
Ryuya Umezawa
Naoki Okayama
Kiyoaki Takeda
Kazuyo Nishida
Natalia Sanz Lavina
Maurizio Mucciola
Maria-Chiara Piccinelli
Nienming Chengå
Miruna Ileana Constantinescu
Hajime Kita

Masaru Shuku
Kimio Suzuki
Taku Nishikawa
Zhi Xiong Chan
Naofumi Takaoka

PARIS

Kengo Kuma
Nicolas Moreau
Sarah Markert
Matthieu Wotling
Louise Lemoine
Sawa Iwasada-Louvel
Elise Fauquembergue
Shinku Noda
Felicien Duval

Bibliography

WRITINGS

10 Houses. Tokyo: Toso Publishing, 1986. Republished in paperback by Chikuma Publishing, 1990. Available in Chinese translation.

Anti-Object: Dissolution and Disintegration of Architecture. Tokyo: Chikuma Publishing, 2000. Available in English translation.

Beyond the Architectural Crisis. Tokyo: Toto Publishing, 1995.

Catastrophe of Architectural Desire. Tokyo: Shin'yosha, 1994.

Defeated Architecture. Tokyo: Iwanami Shoten, 2004. Available in Chinese translation.

Introduction to Architecture: History and Ideology. Tokyo: Chikuma Publishing, 1994.

Kengo Kuma: A Natural Architecture. Tokyo: Iwanami Shoten, 2008.

Lecture and Dialogue. INAX Publishing, 2007.

Shin Toshi-ron Tokyo (A New Debate on Cities). Tokyo: Shueisha Publishing, 2008. Coauthored with Yumi Kiyono.

MONOGRAPHS

Alini, Luigi. *Kengo Kuma: Liticita Contemporanee. Da Stone Museum a Stone Pavilion.* Libria, Italy, 2008.

——. *Kengo Kuma: Opere e Progetti.* Milan: Mondadori Electa, 2005.

——. *Kengo Kuma: Works and Projects.* Milan: Mondadori Electa, 2006.

Bognar, Botond. *Kengo Kuma: Selected Works.* New York: Princeton Architectural Press, 2005.

Fischer, Volker and Ulrich Schneider. *Kengo Kuma: Breathing Architecture.* Germany: Birkhäuser, 2008.

"Kengo Kuma." *GA Architect* (Tokyo) 19, 2005.

Kengo Kuma: Geometries of Nature. Milan: L'Arca Edizioni, 1999.

Kengo Kuma: The Japan Architect 38. Tokyo: Shinkentiku-sha, 2000.

Kengo Kuma. Rome: Edil Stampa, 2006.

Kuma, Kengo. "Kengo Kuma: Digital Gardening." *Space Design.* Tokyo: Kajima Publishing, 1997.

Kuma, Kengo. *Kengo Kuma: Materials, Structures, Details.* Basel: Birkhäuser, 2004.

List of Works

1988

Kyodo Grating, Setagaya-ku, Tokyo (with Satoko
    Shinohara/Spatial Design Studio)
Small Bathhouse in Izu, Kamo-gun, Shizuoka Prefecture
    (with Satoko Shinohara/Spatial Design Studio)

1989

GT-M, Maebashi, Gunma Prefecture (with CAD Institute
    for Planning)

1991

Rustic, Shinjuku-ku, Tokyo
Maiton Resort, Maiton Island in Phuket, Thailand
    (with Spatial Design Studio)
Doric, Minato-ku, Tokyo
M2, Setagaya-ku, Tokyo

1992

Kinjo Golf Club, Soja, Okayama Prefecture
Japan (JR) Museum, Minato-ku, Tokyo

1994

Man-Ju, Sawara-ku, Fukuoka Prefecture
Yusuhara Visitor's Center, Yusuhara, Takaoka-gun,
    Kochi Prefecture
Kiro-san Observatory, Yoshiumi, Ochi-gun, Ehime
    Prefecture

1995

Water/Glass, Atami, Shizuoka Prefecture
Space Design of the Venice Biennale Japanese Pavilion,
    Venice, Italy

1996

Glass/Shadow Golf Club, Tomioka, Miyagi Prefecture
Noh Stage in the Forest, Tome-gun, Miyagi Prefecture
River/Filter, Tamakawa, Fukuoka Prefecture
Moving Garden Civic Hall, Nagaoka, Niigata Prefecture
Nagaoka Culture Forum, Nagaoka, Niigata Prefecture
Kansai-kan National Diet Library, Kyoto
Grass Net, Milan Triennale, Italy

1997

Eco Particle Miyako-jima, Osaka
Simple Garden Hotel, Le Landes, France
Reverse Theater, Chofu, Tokyo
Grass/Glass tower, Tokyo
Yonezawa Public University Project, Yonezawa,
    Yamagata Prefecture
Ocean/City, Heng Qin Island, China
Memorial Park Takasaki, Gunma Prefecture

1998

Awaji Service Area, Awaji, Tsuna-gun, Hyogo Prefecture
Water/Slats, Oiso, Kanagawa Prefecture
EXPO 2005, Basic Conception, Seto, Aichi Prefecture
Seaside Subcenter of Tokyo, Minato-ku, Tokyo

1999

Wood/Slats, Hayama, Miura-gun, Kanagawa Prefecture
Kitakami Canal Museum, Ishinomaki, Miyagi Prefecture
Super Street, Kobe, Hyogo Prefecture
Bamboo House, Kanagawa Prefecture

2000

Ando Hiroshige Museum, Bato-machi, Nasu,
    Tochigi Prefecture
Takayanagi Community Center, Takayanagi,
    Niigata Prefecture
Sakushin Gakuin University, Utsunomiya, Tochigi
    Prefecture
Makuhari Housing Complex, Makuhari, Chiba Prefecture
Nasu History Museum, Nasu, Nasu-gun Tochigi
    Prefecture
Institute of Disaster Prevention, Fujishiro, Kitasoma-
    gum, Ibaraki Prefecture
Bamboo House 2, Nishinomiya, Hyogo Prefecture
Stone Museum, Nasu, Nasu-gun, Tochigi Prefecture

2001

Porous House, Kurakuen Project

Takasaki Parking Building, Takasaki, Gunma Prefecture

Sea/Filter, Onoda, Yamaguchi Prefecture

Ginzan Onsen Hot Spring Bath House, Obanazawa,
    Yamagata Prefecture

The Skin That Filters The River, Minato-ku, Tokyo

Nikko Police Box, Niko, Tochigi Prefecture

2002

Great Bamboo Wall, phase I, Beijing, China

Plastic House, Meguro-ku, Tokyo

Adobe Museum for Wooden Buddha, Shimonoseki,
    Yamaguchi Prefecture

Shochiku Building, Chuo-ku, Tokyo

2003

Housing Exhibition Center

Horai Onsen Bath House, Izu, Shizuoka Prefecture

Forest/Floor, Karuizawa, Nagano Prefecture

Soba Restaurant at Togakushi Shrine, Togakushi,
    Nagano Prefecture

Baiso-in Buddhist Temple, Minato-ku, Tokyo

JR Shibuya Station, facade renovation, Shibuya, Tokyo

One Omotesando, Minato-ku, Tokyo

Paint House Building, Tama, Tokyo

Great Bamboo Wall, phase II, Beijing, China

2004

Masanari Murai Art Museum, Setagaya-ku, Tokyo

Shizuoka Expo Gate Building, Shizuoka Prefecture

Waketokuyama Restaurant, Minato-ku, Tokyo

Shinonome Apartment Building, Koto-ku, Tokyo

Food and Agriculture Museum, Tokyo University of
    Agriculture, the Research Institute of Evolutionary
    Biology, Setagaya-ku, Tokyo

NTT Aoyama Building Renovation Project, Minato-ku,
    Tokyo

LVMH, Chuo-ku, Osaka

Cocon Karasuma, Shimogyo-ku, Kyoto

2005

Fukusaki Hanging Garden, Minato-ku, Osaka

Nagasaki Prefectural Art Museum, Nagasaki, Nagasaki
    Prefecture (with Nikken Sekkei)

Bus Stop in Finland

KxK Pavilion, Hara Museum, Shinagawa-ku, Tokyo

Banraisha, Minato-ku, Tokyo (with Taisei Corporation)

The Scape, Shibuya, Tokyo

Lotus House, East Japan

2006

Y-Hutte, Kuruizawa, Nagano Prefecture

Chokkura Plaza and Shelter, Takanezawa, Tochigi
    Prefecture

Hoshinosato Annex, Kudamatsu, Yamaguchi Prefecture

Ginzan Onsen Fujiya, Obanazawa, Yamagata Prefecture

Z58 Zongtai Box, Shanghai, China

Yusuhara Town Hall, Yusuhara, Kochi Prefecture

2007

Tokyo Midtown Project D North Wing, Minato-ku, Tokyo
    (with Nikkan Kensetsu)

Suntory Museum, Minato-ku, Tokyo (with NTT Facilities)

Modern Teahaus, Frankfurt, Germany

Tobata C Block Project, Kitakyushu, Fukuoka Prefecture
    (with Takenaka Corporation)

Sake No Hana restaurant, London, United Kingdom

Yien East/Archipelago, West Japan

Ondo-cho Civic Center, Kure, Hiroshima Prefecture

2008

Asahi Broadcasting Corporation Headquarters,
    Fukushima-ku, Osaka

Restaunt Kaika-tei, Fukui Prefecture

Shiseikan, Kyoto University of Art and Design,
    Sakyo-ku, Kyoto

JR Hoshakuji Station, Takanezawa, Tochigi Prefecture

Opposite House Hotel, Beijing, China

Jugetsudo Café and Shop, Paris, France

Renovation of Tiffany flagship store in Ginza, Tokyo

UPCOMING PROJECTS

Nezu Art Museum, Minato-ku, Tokyo

Dellis Cay Spa Resort, Turks and Caicos Islands

Suzhou Dwelling Project, Suzhou, China

Tenerife Housing Project

Kenny Heights Museum, Kuala Lumpur, Malaysia

New Sanlitun District Development, Beijing, China

Sanlitun SOHO, Beijing, China

Spiritual Center of Chengdu, Chengdu, China

Chengdu Library, Chengdu, China

Besancon Cultural Centre, Besancon, France

Complex of government buildings related to the area of
    the western railway station of Budapest, Hungary
    (with Peter Janesch and team)

FRAC (Fonds Regional d'Art Contemporain)

Illustration Credits

All drawings and photographs courtesy of Kengo Kuma and Associates,
except as indicated below

Daici Ano: Chokkura Plaza and Shelter, Fukuzaki Hanging Garden,
Ginzan Onsen Fujiya, Hoshinosato Annex, JR Hoshakuji Station, Lotus.House,
LVMH, Nagasaki Prefectural Art Museum, Yien East/Archipelago

Botond Bognar: pp.12–53, 59, 60, 63, 64 right, 91, 119 top left, 136 top left,
143, 144 bottom left and right, 151 bottom, 154 top, 157, 159 top left and right,
160 left, 162, 167, 182 top middle, 183 bottom, 191 top, 196, 197, 198,
234 top middle, 238 top, 244 above right

Imaging Company SS: Cocon Karasuma

Kengo Kuma and Associates: Fuan Teahouse, KxK Pavilion, Modern Teehaus,
Paper Snake, Sake No Hana

Mitsumasa Fujitsuka: Food and Agriculture Museum, Ondo-cho Civic Center,
Oribe Teahouse, Suntory Museum, Yusuhara Town Hall, Z58 Zhongtai Box

Katsuki Miyoshino: Opposite House Hotel, Sanlitun Village South

Masao Nishikawa: Tiffany Ginza

Piczo: Cha Cha Moon

Yoshie Nishikawa: Casa Umbrella

Kouji Okamoto: Tobata C Block

Yoshio Shiratori: Waketokuyama

Yuji Takeuchi: Y-Hutte

Published by
Princeton Architectural Press
37 East Seventh Street, New York, NY 10003

For a free catalog of books, call 1-800-722-6657
Visit our web site at www.papress.com

© 2009 Princeton Architectural Press
All rights reserved
Printed and bound in China
12 11 10 09 4 3 2 1 First edition

Editor: Laurie Manfra
Designer: Paul Wagner

Special thanks to: Nettie Aljian, Sara Bader, Nicola Bednarek, Janet Behning,
Becca Casbon, Carina Cha, Penny (Yuen Pik) Chu, Carolyn Deuschle,
Russell Fernandez, Pete Fitzpatrick, Wendy Fuller, Jan Haux, Clare Jacobson,
Erin Kim, Aileen Kwun, Nancy Eklund Later, Linda Lee, John Myers,
Katharine Myers, Dan Simon, Andrew Stepanian, Jennifer Thompson,
Joseph Weston, and Deb Wood of Princeton Architectural Press
—Kevin C. Lippert, publisher

Library of Congress Cataloging-in-Publication Data
Bognar, Botond, 1944–
Material/immaterial : the new work of Kengo Kuma / Botond Bognar. – 1st ed.
     p.   cm.
Includes bibliographical references.
ISBN 978-1-56898-874-0 (hardcover : alk. paper) –
ISBN 978-1-56898-779-8 (pbk. : alk. paper)
1. Kuma, Kengo, 1954–Themes, motives. 2. Architecture–Japan–History–21st
century. I. Kuma, Kengo, 1954– II. Title. III. Title: a Material immaterial.
NA1559.K77A4 2009
720.92–dc22
                              2009012269